Convinced
by Scripture

'Of all the colourful characters in the Church's history, Martin Luther is probably the most dramatic: fiery, controversial, hilarious and outrageous. Andy Johnston's clear, warm and humorous pocket guide will show you the man as well as the theology.'

Andrew Wilson, pastor and author

'Here is Luther in all his earthy humanity, but through it all the wonder of the gospel shines. This book will stir your interest in one of history's great characters but, more than this, it will stir your faith and your gratitude for the good news he proclaimed.'

Glen Scrivener, evangelist and director of Speak Life

'I really like this brief, colourful and compelling introduction to one of God's world changers. It's written with the enthusiasm and insight I'd expect from Andy. I recommend it, whether you're new to Luther or more familiar.'

Joel Virgo, senior pastor at
Church of Christ the King, Brighton

'This is a gem of a book by a first class Reformation scholar. If you want a concise and compelling treatment of Luther's life and legacy this is the best! We desperately need, in the Church today, to rediscover Luther's joy and confidence in the Gospel of the Grace of God and the authority of 'God's Word written'. This little book will be a big help in that critical need.'

Bishop Wallace Benn

Foreword by Michael Reeves

Convinced
by Scripture

The Life of Martin Luther

Andy Johnston

British Library Cataloguing in Publication Data
A record for this book is available from the British Library

ISBN: 978-1-911272-46-5

Designed and typeset by Pete Barnsley (CreativeHoot)

Printed in the UK by CPI

10Publishing, a division of 10ofthose.com
Unit C, Tomlinson Road, Leyland, Lancashire, PR25 2DY, England

Email: info@10ofthose.com
Website: www.10ofthose.com

Contents

Foreword 1

Introduction 3

1. The boy 7

2. The monk 13

3. The theologian 19

4. The justified sinner 25

5. The reformer 31

6. The 'heretic' 39

7. The Bible translator 55

8. Against the fanatics 63

9. The Church builder 69

10. The family man 81

11. The flawed character 89

12. The legacy 97

Foreword

It was Reformers like Martin Luther that saved my life. I was about twenty years old when the crisis of faith hit. I found myself doubting everything: what to believe, and how to be saved. And nobody I knew seemed to have the answers. So I turned to books and found myself reading Luther. And there I found a soul-mate. Here in this man, born nearly five hundred years before me, was someone who understood, who seemed to share my doubts and fears. But he also had answers – glorious answers! He showed me a gracious God who saves failures simply because he is kind.

It seemed almost too good to be true. I wanted to know: can I really believe that this good news I'm reading in the Bible is actually from God Himself? And as I wrestled with that question, I stumbled across another Reformation figure: John Owen. He showed me that the Bible really does prove itself in a multitude of ways to be God's trustworthy and very own word.

There were others too. Browsing my way through a dusty second-hand bookshop in central London I came across other men of the Reformation, great preachers like Richard Sibbes and Jonathan Edwards. Sibbes showed me the beauty of Christ in a way I'd never seen before, and Edwards the sheer pleasure of knowing God.

It was Luther and the Reformers that God used to bring me out of my dark despair and into a growing happiness in God. And I know I am far from being the only one to have walked that path. So I am keen as mustard on getting others to know the man and his mind. Far from being a mere curiosity for the history books, still today Luther has the ability to make Christians come alive – indeed, to make them roar with laughter at the outrageous graciousness of God. This is a book that introduces Luther well, and I pray it will bring you and many others to enjoy more deeply his extraordinary Gospel discoveries.

Michael Reeves,
President and Professor of Theology at Union School of Theology and author of several books including *Enjoy Your Prayer Life*

Introduction

'My people are destroyed for lack of knowledge'

HOSEA 4:6

In a culture in which I have several Bibles on my bookshelves and a multitude of translations on my mobile phone, it is difficult to imagine how far to the margins of Christian life the Bible had been pushed in the Middle Ages.

Bibles were simply not available in any form at all before the invention of printing and the publication of the Gutenberg Bible in the 1450s. Moreover, the Bible which was available in this period was in Latin, utterly incomprehensible to the vast majority of people. St Jerome's Latin translation, the Vulgate, had been used by the Western Church for over a thousand years. But this was the language of a small educated elite, not that of ordinary people. What is more, probably as few as 5–10% of the population could read at all, even in their own language. Not even all parish priests were literate.

Bearing this in mind, it is not difficult to imagine just how poor the typical sermon was at unpacking the truth of Scripture. Although preaching was a part of the responsibility of the local parish priest, it was by no means top of his job description. Other responsibilities such as the administration of the sacraments of the Church ranked much higher. When he did preach a sermon, it would not be the exposition of a Biblical text but, much more likely, an exhortation to good conduct and works of charity.

The movement that Martin Luther began in 1517 put the Bible back centre stage in the life of the individual believer and in the Church as a whole. The Ninety-Five Theses which he nailed to the church doors in Wittenberg on 31st October 1517, thus beginning the Protestant Reformation, begin with a Bible quote:

'When our Lord and Master Jesus Christ said, "Repent" (Mt 4:17) He willed the entire life of believers to be one of repentance.'

When Luther stood on trial before the Emperor Charles V at the Diet of Worms in 1521, his defence, fundamentally, was an appeal to Scripture:

'Unless I am convicted by scripture and plain reason – I do not accept the authority of the popes and councils, for they have contradicted each other – my conscience is captive to the Word of God. I cannot and I will not recant anything for to go against conscience is neither right nor safe. God help me. Amen.'

A year later, after an intense period of study, Luther published his German New Testament, a pocket-sized book that put the words of Scripture into a language and a format accessible to ordinary literate Germans.

Twelve years later he completed his task and published a whole Bible.

Furthermore, as a pastor, Luther preached over 3,000 sermons, interpreting and applying the Biblical text into the hearts and lives of the people of Wittenberg.

Take the Bible out of Luther's hands and we are left with no Reformation at all. The movement that Luther unleashed in 1517 was a reform of the Church which sought to put the Bible right back at the heart of Christian faith. The Bible was important not simply because it is authoritative, though Luther was in no doubt on this point whatsoever. Scripture was important for Luther because it is a revelation of Christ. As early as 1515 Luther preached a sermon in which he said:

> 'He who would read the Bible must simply take heed that he does not err, for the Scripture may permit itself to be stretched and led, but let no one lead it according to his own inclinations but let him lead it to the source, that is, the cross of Christ. Then he will surely strike the centre.'

Five hundred years later, our culture is arguably even more Biblically illiterate than late medieval society. Scripture is more readily available, but is no more understood or lived out by large numbers of people. If we are to see the re-evangelization of Europe in our day, it will take a similar commitment and clarity to that of Luther. Like Luther, we need to see Scripture as the ultimate fixed reference point. This is not simply a theological statement of faith, but a conviction to live and ultimately to die for. Likewise, we need to preach a message, not simply to our churches, but to the whole of our culture and society that showcases the crucified Messiah in all the Scriptures. Like Luther, we need to put the Cross right back at the heart of Christian faith.

CHAPTER 1

THE BOY

'When God wants to speak with us he does not avail Himself of an angel but of parents'

LUTHER

On 31ˢᵗ October 1517 a 33-year-old university professor nailed a series of theological propositions and arguments to the doors of the church in the small German city where he lived. In doing so, he was imagining he would spark a debate in academic and ecclesiastical circles. In actual fact he changed Europe and ultimately the world. Today there are over 800 million people across the globe who could be described as 'Protestant' in one way or another. The stranglehold on Christian faith exercised by the Roman Catholic Church through the ministry of the priesthood was broken forever and the Bible became a book that was open to all to read and explore. The city was Wittenberg in Saxony, eastern Germany, and the university professor was Martin Luther.

Luther was born on 10th November 1483 in Eisleben, a small Saxon town with a population of only a few thousand. His early years were entirely unremarkable and there is nothing in his childhood that might lead us to imagine his future significance. Catholic opponents writing fifty years after his birth spread the story that his mother had had sex with the Devil to spawn a heretical monster. In fact, Luther's father and mother were entirely ordinary. They were good Catholics; he was baptized the day after he was born on St Martin's Day, hence his name. His father, Hans, was of peasant stock but had done well for himself and had become a copper smelter. When Martin was only three years old the family moved to Mansfeld and there his father continued to climb the social ladder, serving as a town councillor. When he died in 1530 Hans would leave a sizeable sum of money in his will. Luther's mother, Margarethe, invested most of her energies caring for the large family. Martin was the second of five children who survived into adulthood. He had a brother, Jacob, and three sisters.

Growing up as a small boy in the 1490s was very different from childhood today. Corporal punishment from parents and schoolteachers alike was part and parcel of everyday life. Both Martin's mother and his father exercised firm discipline when he stepped out of line. Luther recalled later in life how once 'for the sake of stealing a nut, my mother once beat me until the blood flowed'. Hans was no more easy-going. On one occasion he whipped his son so hard that he ran away and for some while after the young boy was full of anger and resentment towards his father. That Luther was a young boy with a well-developed and tender conscience should come as no surprise – his life as a young adult in the monastery in Erfurt displays similar traits.

In keeping with his increasing social status, Hans was ambitious for his eldest son, hoping that one day Martin might become a lawyer. Hans therefore ensured that Luther went to the best local schools in Mansfeld, Madgeberg and Eisenach. Living away from home for much of the time, Luther was well cared for by various members of his extended family. However, the classroom experience was far from a happy one. He was a quiet and studious boy, but even his natural intelligence did not mean he avoided the barbaric teaching methods of the age. He spoke of his schooling later in adult life as something between purgatory and hell. Failure in Latin drills resulted in the teacher making use of the rod and any one pupil could be beaten up to fifteen times a week. Conversing in German rather than Latin meant being made to wear a donkey mask until another student made the same mistake.

The Church played a hugely important role in Luther's life as a small boy just as it did for all Catholics living in late-medieval Europe. Every baptized man, woman and child was a Christian. Only those who were Jewish by birth, heretical by persuasion or practising witches were not considered to be part of the universal or 'Catholic' Church. The supernatural was accepted as a normal part of everyday life. Fairies and goblins, demons, saints and angels all played their part in the world order whether for good or for ill. The Christian faith was altogether more 'earthy', physical and tangible than it has become. Luther grew up in a world where the relics (bones and material remains of saints) and other 'holy objects' held miraculous powers. Luther's own ruler, Duke Frederick the Wise of Saxony, held the largest collection of relics (over 19,000!) in the whole world. He had gone on pilgrimage to the Holy Land as a young man and had come back with the thumb of his favourite saint, Anna, the mother of the Virgin Mary. To this he added a whole host of bizarre objects which were believed to have miraculous powers – a tooth of St Jerome, four body parts of St Augustine, seven parts of the veil of the Virgin Mary which had been spattered by the blood of Christ, a piece of the infant Jesus' swaddling clothes together with some of the gold and myrrh given by the Wise Men, a strand of Christ's beard and even a twig from the burning bush! A viewing of these objects together with the necessary financial contribution would reduce time in purgatory (see below) for up to 2 million years! To us such paraphernalia seems almost laughable. To people living in late medieval Europe they were part and parcel of the salvation process.

To Luther as a young boy Jesus Christ was first and foremost the judge of the whole universe. He was terrifying in His wrath and fierce in His condemnation of sin. Far from being the mediator between God and man that Paul describes in 1 Timothy 2:5, Christ Himself needed someone to mediate between Himself and sinful human beings. This was where the saints, and particularly the Virgin Mary, came in. Their merits and righteousness had created a surplus 'pool' of grace which could be accessed through indulgences which were granted by the Church. Technically speaking, indulgences were granted by the Church (or even purchased) as an alternative to having to perform an act of penance. Ordinary people, however, had come to believe that salvation could be purchased through indulgences – the ultimate 'prosperity Gospel' message! You could even buy indulgences for your dead loved ones who might well be languishing in purgatory. Purgatory is taught nowhere in the Bible, but verses from the Apocrypha (2 Maccabees 12:43–46) had led the Catholic Church to teach that there was a middle place between Heaven and Hell where you could be purified from your sin before entry into Heaven. In a society where infant mortality rates were sky high, the pressure as a parent to buy an indulgence in order to ensure that your dead infant reached Heaven at the earliest available opportunity was enormous.

Luther and his family were devout in every respect in their faith. As serious-minded Catholics, the high point of their worship was attendance at Mass. This was the service at which the bread and wine became the body and blood of Christ through the miracle of transubstantiation. The priest stood with his back to the congregation reciting the service in Latin and, as he got to the words *'Hoc est corpus meum'* (this is my body), the bread or host, as it was called, was offered up to God as a re-enactment of the sacrifice of Christ at Calvary. Various people in the fourteenth and fifteenth centuries had challenged both the popular superstition surrounding relics, saints and pilgrimages and the high theology of the Mass. Luther took it all at face value. He seems, as far as we can tell, to have been a good pious Catholic boy.

CHAPTER 2

THE MONK

'If ever a monk got to heaven by his monkery, it was me'

LUTHER

In the summer of 1505 Luther was travelling on the road from Mansfeld to Erfurt. Life was good. He had been home to visit his family and was returning to university where he was studying Law. An illustrious career lay ahead of him. As he reached the village of Stotternheim a violent thunderstorm rolled in. Deep in the forest a sense of foreboding and gloom came upon him. Luther, like most people of his time, believed that thunderstorms and other natural phenomenon were signs of God's divine judgment and displeasure. Suddenly, as he took shelter, a bolt of lightning hit a tree right next to where he was standing. Luther was terrified and feared for his life. He cried out 'Dear God! Help me St Anne, I will become a monk!'

St Anne was both the patron saint of miners and, according to legend, the grandmother of Jesus. In invoking such an important saint, Luther was responding like any other devout Catholic of his time. His father was furious with him for his resolution to become a monk, however. Hans had known the struggles and hardships of poverty in his early life but had climbed the social ladder to a position of moderate wealth and security. He had then invested considerable sums of money into his son's schooling and university fees and lodging, no doubt basking in the reflected glory of Martin's achievements and future prospects as a lawyer. All this was now in serious jeopardy.

Ignoring his parents' objections, Luther presented himself at the Augustinian friary in Erfurt two weeks later. The Augustinians were a strict order and this was probably what appealed to Luther about them. He was not looking for a life of ease and pleasure, but rather was trying to do everything he possibly could to secure and guarantee the salvation of his soul. However, the next seven years proved to be the unhappiest in Luther's life. He embraced the monastic life enthusiastically and wholeheartedly. During the cold winter nights he nearly froze to death on occasions because he refused blankets and he nearly starved himself to death, such was his commitment to fasting. The problem for Luther was not what he was required to do physically but what was required of him spiritually.

According to the school of thought that Luther was trained in, salvation was the result of a co-operation between our human efforts and the grace of God. Over a thousand years earlier the great Church Father Augustine of Hippo (354–430) had roundly condemned as heretical the self-help attempts at salvation offered by the British monk Pelagius (c390–418). However, his ideas, known as 'Pelagianism', or at least a diluted version of them, had once again reared their ugly head in the Church. Luther came to believe that his salvation could only be secured as a result of him maximizing his efforts to please God. As God saw him acting in this way, straining with every fibre of his being to do his very best, then God would give him the grace that was needed to be accepted by a holy God. Righteousness came, according to this line of thinking, as a combination of human endeavour and the grace of God.

The big question for Luther was what did it mean to do one's very best? A range of possibilities were open to the Christian faithful at this time. There were pilgrimages to go on and opportunities to visit the holiest shrines in all of Christendom. There were indulgences which could be purchased and intercessions which could be made to the saints. Best of all, he could avail himself of the seven sacraments of the Church through which the priesthood ministered the grace of God to the Christian faithful. These were baptism, communion, penance, the last rites, marriage, confirmation and holy orders. For Luther it was the regular receiving of communion through the Mass and confession of sin through the sacrament of penance that were particularly important as tools whereby the grace of God was accessed on a regular and ongoing basis.

For Luther the system was a living nightmare. It was impossible for him to know the joy of receiving grace because, no matter how hard he tried, his good works were never 'good enough'. God's grace was therefore unattainable. He kept the rules of his order as diligently as he knew how. He fasted, he prayed, he read and he did everything else he could possibly do that might be thought of as a 'good work' but none of it was good enough. It was all tainted by his sin and shortcomings.

Conscious both of his sin and of God's holiness, Luther felt he was living through Hell itself. If Hell is about suffering, punishment and a sense of forsakenness, then Luther was enduring Hell on earth. On a daily basis he lived with the reality that God was angry with his sin. Looking back later in life, able to reflect with a much stronger affinity with the Scriptures than he had in his twenties, he interpreted his suffering through the lens of David's experience in Psalm 31. He felt an immediate affinity with David who testifies to a life of sorrow and his body wasting away (verse 10). His sin meant that he was cut off from the sight of God (verse 22).

Two years after entering the monastery, Luther was ordained to the priesthood. Far from bringing solutions to the crisis of his faith, this brought only fresh terrors. He now had the responsibility of bringing Heaven to earth through the sacrament of communion. He was afforded a privilege that was not even given to the angels. As he said the words of the Mass the bread and wine were transformed miraculously into the body and blood of Christ and then lifted up as an offering for sin. This was utterly overwhelming. Luther was overpowered by his own sin, his guilt and the holiness of God. To stand before human royalty (which Luther in fact did in 1521) is one thing, but to stand before the King of Heaven, surrounded by angels, at whose word the whole earth trembles, was unspeakably daunting.

Confession, known as the sacrament of penance, was another of the treasured ceremonies of the Church that did little to offer any comfort or hope to Luther in his need. He spent sometimes as many as six hours confessing his sin, or at least every sin he could think of, to his confessor John Staupitz, the Augustinian Vicar-General. However, this brought him no relief from the burden of guilt and condemnation he carried.

In 1510 Luther had another opportunity for spiritual comfort and consolation. He was chosen to go to Rome to settle a dispute that had arisen within the Augustinian order. As with the Mass and confession, he hoped that this experience might provide him with the spiritual certainties he was so lacking. To visit the seat of the Bishop of Rome, the Pope, the Vicar of Christ on earth was surely going to be a high point in his spiritual journey. But he was disillusioned on every level. The Italian priests were frivolous, incompetent and some were downright irreverent and immoral. Luther was particularly shocked at vice and prostitution in the 'holy city'. He later remarked, 'If there is a Hell then Rome is built on it.'

Luther had celebrated the Mass with awe and reverence, believing with deep conviction that the bread and wine were miraculously transformed into the body and blood of Christ. But here he found priests declaring 'Bread thou art and bread thou shalt remain'. As he climbed the *Scala Sancta*, the twenty-eight stairs that had supposedly once stood in front of Pontius Pilate's palace, he did so on his hands and knees, praying the Lord's Prayer on every step, and kissing each one in the hope that this might release his grandfather from purgatory. But when he got to the top he pondered, 'Who knows if this is true?'

If Luther could not secure his own salvation through medieval religion, it was not through want of trying. However, it was not mere disgust at the abuses of Rome that pushed him towards his challenge to the authority of the Pope. Over the next few years he began to study the Bible more and more and this was to lead to a transformation in his understanding of his relationship with God.

CHAPTER 3

THE THEOLOGIAN

'I swear to defend evangelical truth vigorously'

LUTHER, RECEIVING HIS DOCTOR OF THEOLOGY DEGREE

IN 1512

By 1512 Luther was at breaking point. The semi-Pelagian theology which had so shaped his thinking had led him to such a place of despair and anguish that he was utterly convinced of his own eternal damnation. His father-confessor John Staupitz, concerned about Luther's well-being and even his sanity, offered him an alternative to day-to-day monastic life. Luther was appointed as Professor of Biblical Studies at the newly created University of Wittenberg.

Founded as recently as 1502, Wittenberg lacked the prestige of older universities like Cologne (1388), Louvain (1425) or the Sorbonne, Paris (1257). It was financed by the huge collection of relics that Duke Frederick the Wise had gathered. The relics brought pilgrims and pilgrims brought revenue as the Christian faithful would pay to venerate the relics and thus reduce the time they and their dead loved ones spent in purgatory. In the next ten years Luther devised a theology that ultimately came to destroy not only his university's source of funding but the entire fabric of medieval Christianity.

Luther's theological diet before academic life was largely shaped by self-help semi-Pelagianism, but this was not the only influence on him. His mentor, John Staupitz, had encouraged him to read the German Christian medieval mystical writers. Luther imbibed the sermons of John Tauler (c1300–1361), a Dominican monk who taught that the state of the soul was more affected by a personal relationship with God than by external practices. At the same time, Luther also came across another book, the *Theologia Germanica*, which he wrongly believed had been written by Tauler as it expressed many similar sentiments. It taught that the Christian life was one of a renouncing of sin as a means of allowing our own will to be replaced by God's. Luther was so impressed that he published his own edited version of the *Theologia Germanica* in 1516. He claimed at the time that

> *'Next to the Bible and St. Augustine, no book has ever come into my hands from which I have learned more of God and Christ, and man and all things that are.'*

The strength of medieval mysticism at this phase of Luther's life can be seen in another of his earliest works, the *Seven Penitential Psalms* (1517).

Now that he was an academic theologian, Luther also began to study the writings of the great early Church Father Augustine of Hippo (354–430) more and more intensively. As he did so, this began to significantly influence his view of God, sin, human beings and the grace of God. The semi-Pelagian notion that human beings were capable, by their own efforts, of achieving a status whereby God would impart His grace would have been abhorrent to Augustine. Augustine had a strong view of the sovereignty of God, of the inherent sinfulness of man (original sin) and the complete inability of human beings to do anything that could possibly contribute to their salvation.

Later on in his life, once Luther had come to his fully formed view of justification by faith alone, Luther believed that he had essentially rediscovered Augustine. In fact, Luther went much further than Augustine or any other medieval theologian for that matter. Augustine believed that man was essentially in a process, through the grace of God, of being made righteous. Luther, by contrast, completely separated the process of sanctification from the act of justification. Sanctification is the work of the Holy Spirit in the life of the believer that causes us to be conformed to the image of Christ. Justification, far from being a process, is a single instantaneous action whereby we are credited with the righteousness of Christ won for us through that once-for-all sacrifice for sin at Calvary.

However, the most important influence on Luther's theology in this period was clearly the Bible. As Professor of Biblical Studies he began first to read and research the text of Scripture and then, in turn, to teach his findings to his students. In 1514–15 he lectured on the Psalms and then in turn on the letters to the Romans (1515–16), the Galatians (1516–17) and the Hebrews (1517–18).

Luther had begun to study the Bible seriously as early as 1509, but now he pored over the text day and night. He mainly used Jerome's Latin (Vulgate) translation, but was also growing in his knowledge of the Hebrew of the Old Testament and, in particular, the Greek of the New. In 1516 the Dutch reformer Erasmus published his Greek New Testament giving Luther and other Biblical scholars easy access to a reliable text of the original language of the New Testament for the first time.

Writing in 1545 near the end of his life, Luther implied that his fully formed position on justification by faith alone which he came to in reading Romans 1:16–17 came in an instantaneous moment. In fact, it is better viewed as the final destination in a long journey of discovery and exploration of the Scriptures. He began a theological journey in 1512 on the issues of sin, righteousness and grace that probably only reached its fullest conclusion as late as 1519.

Luther loved the Bible. He read through it from cover to cover roughly every six months. He pored over the Biblical text, hour upon hour. He compared the Bible to a mighty tree and every word of it to little twigs, claiming that he had 'knocked on every one of these twigs to discover what they might be able to teach [me]'. His method was thoroughly scholarly and involved thorough investigation of the meaning of every word in the text. But the aim was to combine academic method with prayer and meditation so that Christ, the Word of God made flesh, might be encountered through the written words of the text. As he read and taught over a five or six-year period, his views began to change. His work on the Psalms did not change his view that God is the judge of the entire universe, but this view began to be balanced with a growing awareness of the mercy of God. All of this was to reach a climax as he explored Paul's letter to the Romans. Romans as the fullest explanation of the Gospel in the whole of the New Testament was to have profound implications, first in Luther's mind and heart, beyond that in his restatement of what the good news of Jesus really is and, ultimately, in enabling millions of people to come into a living encounter with the grace of God.

CHAPTER 4

THE JUSTIFIED SINNER

*'I felt I had been born again, the gates were open
and I had entered paradise'*

LUTHER IN 1545, RECALLING HIS CONVERSION EXPERIENCE

A year before his death in 1546 Luther, looking back over twenty-five years, recounted how he had come to a fully formed view of justification by faith alone through the saving grace of Christ alone. His years in the monastery had left him with a very negative view of the idea of the justice of God. For him at this stage of his journey, God's justice could only be understood as his judgment of sinners. Acutely aware of his own sin, he felt a deep inner anger at the unfairness and injustice of God. He had dark, blasphemous thoughts and even described himself as hating God. He concluded that the Gospel, far from being the good news that it claimed to be was, in actual fact, profoundly bad news! The Ten Commandments, as the Law of God, reveal the sinfulness of the human heart and therefore threatened God's wrath. The Gospel, far from being 'good news' simply confirmed Luther's worst fears. It was at this point of desperation that Luther re-examined Paul's letter to the Romans:

> 'I meditated night and day on those words until at last, by the mercy of God, I paid attention to their context: "The justice of God is revealed in it, as it is written: 'The just person lives by faith.'" I began to understand that in this verse the justice of God is that by which the just person lives by a gift of God, that is, by faith. I began to understand that this verse means that the justice of God is revealed through the Gospel, but it is a passive justice, i.e. that by which the merciful God justifies us by faith, as it is written: "The just person lives by faith." All at once I felt that I had been born again and entered into paradise itself through open gates. Immediately I saw the whole of Scripture in a different light. I ran through the Scriptures from memory and found that other terms had analogous meanings, e.g., the work of God, that is, what God works in us; the power of God, by which he makes us powerful; the wisdom of God, by which he makes us wise; the strength of God, the salvation of God, the glory of God.'

This was Luther's great 'tower experience' as it became known. His encounter with God through the text of

Scripture changed him from the inside out and has had a similarly powerful effect on millions of Christians since.

How do we make sense of this moment in Luther's life? First, we must remember that Luther is an old man by the time he has recorded his conversion experience. As he grew to appreciate God's work of grace in his heart more and more, the distortion of his memories over time may have led him to forget how gradual the process was, so that he concentrated too much into this one moment.

Second, we see that Luther did not come to a fully formed view of justification by faith alone and then, as a result take on the forces of Roman Catholicism. Rather, Luther was making his discoveries as he was challenging Rome. His publication of the Ninety-Five Theses and the battle that ensued from this occurred as he was still evolving his own views on justification by faith, as well as a whole lot of other issues.

Third, we see how radical Luther's departure from his theological training really was. His reading of Romans 1:17, 'For in [the Gospel] the righteousness of God is revealed from faith for faith, as it is written, "The righteous shall live by faith."' led Luther to turn the semi-Pelagian modern way school of theology on its head. Catholic theologians and even some modern evangelical scholars have accused him of caricaturing late medieval Catholic theology of justification as exclusively semi-Pelagian. They point out that there were a variety of views in the Church at that time about how man is put in a right standing with God. Others, more seriously, have criticized him for misunderstanding what Paul is saying in the first place. Is Paul talking about faith in Christ or the faithfulness of Christ?

All of this begs some fundamental questions. Luther came to understand that the righteousness of God is not simply His perfection and holiness which causes Him to judge human beings for their sinful condition and behaviour. As Luther suggests, this doesn't sound like the good news the Gospel claims to be. Rather righteousness should be understood as a gift acquired only by faith in the saving work of Christ. It is this which puts the believer in right standing with a holy God. This is what Luther called the 'great exchange', our sin exchanged for His righteousness. As he explained in his lectures on the Psalms (1519–21):

> 'That is the mystery which is rich in divine grace to sinners: wherein by a wonderful exchange our sins are no longer ours but Christ's and the righteousness of Christ not Christ's but ours. He has emptied Himself of His righteousness that He might clothe us with it, and fill us with it. And He has taken our evils upon Himself that He might deliver us from them … in the same manner as He grieved and suffered in our sins, and was confounded, in the same manner we rejoice and glory in His righteousness.'

This is surely 'good news' and it is surely at the very heart of the Christian Gospel. In what is arguably the earliest summary of the essentials of Christian faith and therefore the earliest Christian Creed the Apostle Paul begins:

'For I delivered to you as of first importance what I also received: that Christ died for our sins in accordance with the Scriptures...' (1 Corinthians 15:3)

It was this that Luther rediscovered for the Church: namely that Christ's death and His death alone pays for sin and puts us in right standing with God. Grace, the experience of the perfect righteousness of Christ given as a free gift is utterly transformational, releasing us from the duty of religious performance. All of Luther's guilt was gone. He was at last free to know and enjoy a relationship with God as a dearly loved son rather than as a cowering and fearful servant.

CHAPTER 5

THE REFORMER

'As soon as the coin in the coffer rings the soul
from purgatory springs'
ATTRIBUTED TO JOHN TETZEL

In the spring of 1517 Luther heard alarming stories concerning an itinerant indulgence-seller, a Dominican monk named John Tetzel. Tetzel was preaching just over the Saxony border in neighbouring Brandenburg in the towns of Zerbst and Juterbourg. Tetzel was making promises that appealed to vulnerable folk from Wittenberg who had travelled across the border concerned about their own salvation and also of the eternal security of their loved ones. Quoting Bible verses such as Isaiah 55:6 'Seek the LORD while He may be found' and John 9:4 'We must work the works of him who sent me while it is day' for 'night is coming,' Tetzel urged the Christian faithful to buy the indulgences he was selling at the earliest opportunity. Young and old, clergy and laity, rich and poor, married and single – none were exempt from his sales pitch. Only through the means of grace provided by the Church – confession, absolution and satisfaction – could the soul sail through the stormy seas of life and find safety and eternal security in Heaven.

'Whoever has confessed and is contrite and puts his alms in the box ... will have all of his sins forgiven' claimed Tetzel. Perhaps most outrageously of all, he puts the words of Job (19:21) 'Have mercy on me, have mercy on me ... for the hand of God has touched me' into the mouths of dead parents in purgatory to appeal to their living children to buy indulgences to free them from punishment and pain.

As Luther heard the confessions of the local townsfolk, he was greatly perturbed by the promises that had been made to them in Tetzel's preaching. As he examined the indulgences themselves he was only further agitated. Luther was both a pastor and a theologian-teacher. He was angered on both fronts by Tetzel's activities.

Luther had become concerned as early as 1515 that indulgences had the potential to cheapen grace. In the popular imagination they had come to be equated with forgiveness of sin. Indulgences were part and parcel of the 'sacrament of penance', one of the seven ceremonies in the Catholic Church which were a means of distributing grace to the Christian faithful. Penance was broken down into three distinct parts – confession of sin, absolution (in which the priest proclaimed forgiveness) and an act of penance or 'satisfaction for sin'. This 'satisfaction' could range from saying some prayers for a minor sin, to long pilgrimages or self-inflicted punishments for severe sins. The purchase of an indulgence was a replacement for an act of penance. It was not quite a promise of forgiveness for money, but it was not a million miles away. Throw the offer of release from purgatory for dead relatives for the purchase of an indulgence into the mix and a 'coin in the coffer' became a useful marketing jingle for Tetzel's campaign.

Tetzel's indulgences had the word 'scam' written all over them as far as Luther was concerned. He saw a financial rather than spiritual motive as the main driver behind Tetzel's ministry. It expressed some of the worst excesses of late medieval Catholicism at both the highest and lowest levels.

The sale of the particular papal plenary indulgence that Tetzel was marketing had been permitted in Brandenburg because the local prince-bishop, Albert of Hohenzollern was in serious debt. He had recently purchased the office of Archbishop of Mainz. In itself, this was not necessarily unusual. Purchase of high clerical office, known as 'simony' after Simon the Sorcerer's attempts to buy spiritual power (Acts 8:9–24) was sometimes frowned upon but could be a useful source of revenue. Albert had paid Pope Leo X the huge sum of 31,000 ducats for his confirmation in post. Not having the necessary liquid cash, Albert had borrowed the money from a powerful Austrian banking family. He was being charged 20% interest and so was under pressure to repay the loan as soon as possible. He therefore reached a deal with Leo to sell a papal indulgence in his territories. Half the money was to go on the repayment of the loan and the remainder went straight into papal coffers. Leo too was under financial pressure – he was in the middle of a vast rebuilding project, the new St Peter's Basilica in Rome which had been begun by his predecessor, Julius II.

The background to Tetzel's campaign – ambitious popes, greedy bankers, powerful nobles, the purchase of spiritual office – might lead us to conclude that Luther's Reformation was a product of the abuses and corruption of late medieval Catholicism. But Luther was more theologically driven and pastorally motivated. Essentially he was spotting theological problems. The very first of the Ninety-Five Theses set the tone for his whole argument:

'1. When our Lord and Master Jesus Christ said, "Repent" (Mt 4:17), he willed the entire life of believers to be one of repentance.'

Luther was not rejecting penance at this point. Yet he was calling into question the medieval obsession with the sacrament itself and calling for a much more radical change of heart and life in the believer. Luther's other objections do not look particularly remarkable either. He does not reject the existence of purgatory at this point; rather he takes it for granted. Neither does he challenge the authority of the papacy or of Catholicism as an institution. At this point in his life Luther claimed to be a loyal son of the Church and there is no reason to disbelieve him. Even the articles below which are amongst some of the boldest statements in the document are hardly revolutionary:

'2. This word [repent] cannot be understood as referring to the sacrament of penance, that is, confession and satisfaction, as administered by the clergy.

27. They preach only human doctrines who say that as soon as the money clinks into the money chest, the soul flies out of purgatory.

28. It is certain that when money clinks in the money chest, greed and avarice can be increased; but when the church intercedes, the result is in the hands of God alone.

32. Those who believe that they can be certain of their salvation because they have indulgence letters will be eternally damned, together with their teachers.

35. They who teach that contrition is not necessary on the part of those who intend to buy souls out of purgatory or to buy confessional privileges preach unchristian doctrine.

36. Any truly repentant Christian has a right to full remission of penalty and guilt, even without indulgence letters.

41. Papal indulgences must be preached with caution, lest people erroneously think that they are preferable to other good works of love.

42. Christians are to be taught that the Pope does not intend that the buying of indulgences should in any way be compared with works of mercy.

43. Christians are to be taught that he who gives to the poor or lends to the needy does a better deed than he who buys indulgences.

49. Christians are to be taught that papal indulgences are useful only if they do not put their trust in them, but very harmful if they lose their fear of God because of them.

50. Christians are to be taught that if the Pope knew the exactions of the indulgence preachers, he would rather that the basilica of St. Peter were burned to ashes than built up with the skin, flesh, and bones of his sheep.

62. The true treasure of the Church is the most holy Gospel of the glory and grace of God.'

When Luther first posted the Ninety-Five Theses on the church doors in Wittenberg on 31st October 1517 he had no intention of schism with the Roman Catholic Church. He could not have possibly imagined how strongly the Catholic hierarchy would respond to his scholarly inquiries. Luther was merely expressing theological concerns which resulted in pastoral angst about certain aspects of the doctrine and practice of the sale of indulgences.

Luther was doing what any university professor in the

sixteenth century would do when he here was trying to engage in an academic debate. He hand-wrote ninety-five theological statements and propositions in Latin and posted them where other scholars could see, read and respond. The theses became important because of their mass circulation. They were quickly translated into German and printed, first in Nuremberg, and then many times over. What should have been a debate restricted to ivory-towered academics became the talk of every tavern and marketplace in Germany. Shoemakers, furriers, weavers, the lowliest manual workers across Germany began to develop and express theological opinions! Luther quickly became aware of the power and potential of the printed word – going so far as to say that printing was 'God's highest and extremest act of grace whereby the business of the Gospel is driven forward'.

There is no doubt that the 'indulgence controversy' could have been settled quickly had the Pope had a mind to do so. Posterity has left us with two different responses that Leo X is meant to have made when he first heard of Luther and the Ninety-Five Theses. One report has the Pope respond that it was 'Nothing but a monkish squabble' – in other words the controversy was just a dispute between two rival monastic Orders, the Augustinians and the Dominicans. Another report has him saying, 'Luther is a drunken German. He will feel differently when he is sober.' In truth, Leo probably said neither of these things but he certainly failed spectacularly in any attempt to deal with the problem. Luther had raised serious theological concerns which could not be dismissed as simply religious tribalism or nationalism. Instead of addressing Luther's concerns, modifying the doctrine of indulgences and correcting the worst abuses, the Catholic Church decided that it would raise the stakes. This was not, the Pope's defenders argued, a quarrel about indulgences. It was a challenge to the authority of the Church itself and to the Pope in particular. As Luther found himself pushed into this corner, he came out fighting.

CHAPTER 6

THE 'HERETIC'

'I consider Rome to be the throne of Antichrist'

LUTHER'S CONDEMNATION OF THE PAPAL BULL OF 1520
WHICH DECLARED HIM A HERETIC

On 31ˢᵗ October 1517 when he nailed his Ninety-Five Theses to the church doors in Wittenberg, Luther claimed he was 'a loyal son of the Church'. Within four years, however, he had been condemned as a heretic by the papacy and therefore was excommunicated from the Catholic Church. He was declared an outlaw by the Holy Roman Emperor Charles V, meaning he could be shot on sight anywhere in Germany. Why and how did events more so quickly? Did Luther jump or was he pushed?

From an evangelical perspective Luther was no heretic. Rather than deviating from the mainstream, orthodox, Christian faith, Luther was rediscovering the authentic Gospel. His searching of the Scriptures as an academic theologian had led him to conclude that the Church had drifted from her theological moorings into dangerous new territory. Investigation and reading of the Bible was not heretical, nor was it dangerous in the eyes of the Church (except in England) to translate the Bible from the Latin Vulgate into national languages. His view that righteousness came not through performance of good works but as a gift of God through sheer grace pushed the boundaries of what was usual in the medieval Church, but it certainly can't be considered heretical.

Only after Luther's death, at the Council of Trent (1563) did the Catholic Church come to the definitive position that salvation is by faith and works. In Luther's day it was perfectly possible, if a little radical perhaps, to argue for justification by faith alone and be a good orthodox Catholic. The key issue that made Luther a heretic in the minds of conservative-minded Catholics was authority and, in particular, his rejection of the authority of the Pope as Vicar (representative) of Christ on earth and therefore as the supreme arbiter of matters of Christian faith and doctrine.

A year after Luther's publication of the Ninety-Five Theses, he was summoned to appear before the Diet of Augsburg. A 'diet' was a gathering of the German princes, bishops and 'imperial' (i.e. free) cities. This particular meeting was mainly to raise taxes for war on the Ottoman Turks. Leo X had wanted Luther to be tried for heresy in Rome, and this could have meant only one outcome for Luther – condemnation and execution for heresy. Fearing this outcome, Luther's supporters managed to get the venue changed to Augsburg. German soil was safer ground, but by no means completely secure. Luther faced an understandably hostile Church and state and an extremely erudite theological opponent in Cardinal Cajetan in 1518. Cajetan gave Luther a three-day interrogation in which he urged him to recant his 'heresy'. Luther was a heretic in Cajetan's eyes because, in questioning indulgences, he had challenged papal authority since indulgences were issued, after all, on the authority of the Bishop of Rome. Shortly after the diet, the papacy made an official statement (a papal 'bull') which defined the doctrine of indulgences and did eliminate the worst abuses. Clearly Rome was happy to adjust and modify on this point; on the issue of papal authority, however, there was no room for manoeuvre or discussion whatsoever. Battle lines had been drawn.

With the benefit of hindsight, and the knowledge that Luther died of natural causes in 1546, it is easy to minimize the real danger that Luther found himself in at Augsburg. A hearing on German soil was better than a trial in Rome, but it was hardly plain sailing. Luther had hoped for a genuine debate with Cajetan, but was simply given the opportunity to recant his alleged heresies.

When rumours reached Luther that his enemies were planning to arrest him, he was smuggled out of the city under cover of darkness by his supporters. He did not even risk gathering his clothes or riding equipment. He was, quite literally, fleeing for his life.

A year and a half after the publication of the Ninety-Five Theses, Luther was invited to debate his ideas at

Heidelberg in April 1518. Pope Leo X, no doubt spurred on by Cajetan's assertions at Augsburg, was pushing the Augustinian Order hard to condemn Luther and his ideas. However, he made a fundamental error in allowing John Staupitz, Luther's mentor and the head of the Augustinian Order in Germany, to tackle the issue rather than insisting that it be dealt with by Rome directly. Staupitz gave Luther the opportunity to present his ideas to his Augustinian brothers and thus to a wider audience.

At Heidelberg Luther focused his statements not on the more controversial issues about authority in the Church but much more on issues relating to sin, good works, faith, righteousness, grace, suffering and the Cross. Far from presenting Luther in a bad light as the Pope had hoped, Heidelberg only served to enhance Luther's reputation. A young Dominican monk named Martin Bucer, who was later to become a significant evangelical reformer in Strasburg, was in the audience and was spellbound by Luther. Bucer, like many other young theologians at the time was increasingly sceptical of scholastic theology and more and more attracted to Erasmus' Christian humanist reform programme with its emphasis on a return to the Bible in its original languages (Hebrew and Greek) as the purest source of Christian faith and doctrine. Bucer saw an immediate connection between Luther and Erasmus:

'In giving answers his pleasantness was remarkable, in listening his patience was beyond compare, in his

refutation you would have recognized the shrewdness of Paul, not Scotus and, with his replies so concise, so accurate and drawn from the store of divine Scriptures, he easily led them to admire him. The next day I had a private and friendly conversation with the man, remote from observation, and a meal long prepared and desired, not for its food, but its teachings. Whatever question I asked, he explained very lucidly. All his views concurred with Erasmus, except that he seems to excel in this one respect, namely what Erasmus only implies Luther teaches openly. O if only I had the time to write more to you about this.'

The connection was over-played. As events unfolded it became apparent that Luther and Erasmus espoused very different theologies. Nevertheless, Luther's reputation was significantly enhanced by the connection made in people's minds between him and Erasmus and this was even more the case the following year at the Leipzig debate.

The Leipzig debate was a disputation originally between Luther's colleague in the theology faculty at Wittenberg, Andreas Carlstadt and an arch-conservative professor from the University of Ingolstadt, John Eck. Eck was, like John Tetzel, a Dominican monk and thus a natural tribal opponent of Luther. In other respects, however, he was very different. Tetzel was a buffoon; Eck was a highly respected debater and theologian. In the first instance he challenged Carlstadt on the issues that had come to the fore in the Heidelberg disputation, namely free will and grace. However, he then drew Luther into the debate which then broadened to include a much broader range of topics, namely purgatory, indulgences, the sacrament of penance and the biggest issue of all, papal authority. As Luther researched and prepared he found himself adopting an increasingly radical position – and even moved so far as to conclude that the Pope was the Antichrist!

This did not augur well for a theological consensus between him and Eck. During the debate Eck used Scripture to argue for papal authority. His 'proof text' was Matthew 16:18: 'I tell you, you are Peter, and on this rock I will build my church'. The Pope as Bishop of Rome, derived his authority from Peter and ultimately, therefore, from Christ Himself. Luther, on the other hand, whilst willing to recognize the papacy as a divinely ordained institution, rejected the Pope's authority in matters of salvation. Eck was able to manoeuvre Luther to concede that many of his opinions on this issue coincided with those of Jan Hus, a Bohemian theologian and reformer who had been burnt at the stake at the Council of Constance a hundred years earlier. In so doing, Luther claimed that both the councils of the Church and popes could err. Only Scripture was finally authoritative for the Church in matters of doctrine. As far as Eck was concerned, this was game, set and match. Luther was a heretic because he had openly acknowledged that his view of papal authority was the same as that of the condemned heretic Hus.

As with Heidelberg, however, Leipzig served to enhance Luther's popularity and reputation, particularly amongst the younger generation of university academics. Eck may have won the debate, but he had done so using medieval scholastic theology, a style and frame of reference which looked increasingly old-fashioned and out of date. Technically, Luther had lost. But he emerged with an enhanced image and reputation, as someone who fitted the new generation of Christian humanist scholarship.

The road to Luther's formal condemnation as a heretic by the papacy was swift from this point on. On 15th June 1520 Leo X issued the papal bull *Exsurge Domine*. This official condemnation of Luther as a heretic began with a prayer. Alluding to the Song of Solomon (2:15), the Lord is invoked to arise against the foxes that have arisen which seek to destroy the vineyard (i.e. the Church). There are a wide range of Luther's views that are roundly condemned, but his views on the authority (or otherwise) of the papacy occupy centre stage.

'25. The Roman Pontiff, the successor of Peter, is not the Vicar of Christ over all the churches of the entire world, instituted by Christ Himself in blessed Peter.

26. The word of Christ to Peter: "Whatsoever you shall loose on earth," etc., is extended merely to those things bound by Peter himself.

27. It is certain that it is not in the power of the Church or the pope to decide upon the articles of faith, and much less concerning the laws for morals or for good works.

28. If the pope with a great part of the Church thought so and so, he would not err; still it is not a sin or heresy to think the contrary, especially in a matter not necessary for salvation, until one alternative is condemned and another approved by a general Council.'

A year after Luther's condemnation as a heretic by the Pope he was placed under imperial ban by the Holy Roman Emperor Charles V. This meant that in theory at least he could be shot on sight on German soil. Luther had become an outlaw, an international pariah, a sort of sixteenth-century Osama bin Laden.

Between these two condemnations, the first ecclesiastical and the second secular, Luther wrote three books – *The Address to the Christian Nobility of the German Nation* (August 1520), *The Babylonian Captivity of the Church* (September 1520) and *The Freedom of the Christian Man* (November 1520). In these three pamphlets we see Luther at his very best. He was, at this stage of his career, at the very height of his popularity and his creative powers. He was thirty-four years of age and he was the darling of Germany. Students and younger scholars in the universities loved him. He was the talk of almost every marketplace and tavern in Germany. Even those who did not share his theological convictions, like his local prince, Frederick the Wise of Saxony, gave him support because Luther offered them an opportunity to champion the cause of German nationalism against the foreign power of Rome.

In 1519 Charles V, ruler of the Low Countries and Spain was elected Emperor of Germany following the death of his grandfather Maximillian. Within two years Charles had summoned the princes, bishops and cities of Germany to a new diet which began in January 1521, the Diet of Worms. The 'Luther problem' was just one of a number of difficult issues Charles was facing. But in April Luther, having been promised safe passage to and from Worms, was summoned and given the opportunity to confirm or renounce his views. Attendance at Worms was risky, but not half so dangerous as Augsurg had been three years earlier. In 1518, he had been an unknown Augustinian monk suspected of heresy. He had therefore half-expected to die at Augsburg and had been plagued with theological self-doubt. Why should he be right in matters of doctrine when this inevitably implied that the rest of Christendom had been wrong for more than a thousand years? But by 1521 Luther had achieved celebrity status. He attracted support right across the social spectrum – German nationalists, Christian humanists, well-educated citizens of important cities, students and even peasants were becoming attracted to his cause.

When Luther stood before Charles V at the Diet of Worms and was asked to recant the heresies contained in his books he chose not to give a straight 'yes' or 'no' answer. He asked, in the first place, for an extra twenty-four hours to consider his response. The following day Luther chose to divide his writings into three different categories before he gave his answer. The first category, he argued, his devotional books would not even be problematic to his enemies and so required no recantation. The second category included books written against the Pope in which he had attacked false doctrine. He was unable and unwilling to recant these writings since to do so would only serve to strengthen tyranny. The third category involved books written against individuals who had defended Rome. Here Luther concedes that his tone may have been more violent than might be expected from a clergyman but again finds himself unable to recant since to do so would only be to sanction the views of his opponents.

The Freedom of the Christian Man fell largely into category one of Luther's writings. It is devotional rather than polemical in tone. It is the logical outworking and development of his theology of justification by faith alone. Luther concluded that 'a Christian is a perfectly free lord of all, subject to none' because he is saved through grace by faith and not by works. Nevertheless 'a Christian is a perfectly dutiful servant of all, subject to all' and therefore should not look to abuse his freedom but rather use it to serve God wholeheartedly. Luther's emphasis on justification by faith alone has led some critics to see him as someone who saw mankind's relationship with God only through legal and forensic eyes. *The Freedom of the Christian Man* dispels this myth. Much of Luther's emphasis in this beautiful book is on the believer's union with Christ and the primary metaphor for this is marriage. As the bride and groom exchange rings, so our sin is given to Christ and, in return, we receive his perfect righteousness.

The Address to the Christian Nobility of the German Nation and *The Babylonian Captivity of the Church*, however, fell very much into Luther's second category. Both were a direct attack against the false doctrine of the Pope. *The Address to the Christian Nobility* is a book essentially about authority. Luther appeals to powers beyond that of the Pope – to Scripture and to the authority of the general councils of the Church. It is also a book with a distinctly political message for Luther is appealing to nationalist sentiments in the German princes. Citing Revelation 5:10 'You have made them a kingdom and priests to our God' and 1 Peter 2:9 'You are a ... royal priesthood' as counter-arguments, he suggests to the German political classes that they have been hoodwinked by the papacy into believing that they should see themselves as second-class Christians. Luther's rediscovery of the New Testament doctrine of the priesthood of all believers was a powerful weapon against the armoury of the Pope.

'The Romanists have, with great adroitness, drawn three walls round themselves, with which they have hitherto protected themselves, so that no one could reform them, whereby all Christendom has fallen terribly.

Firstly, if pressed by the temporal power, they have affirmed and maintained that the temporal power has no jurisdiction over them, but, on the contrary, that the spiritual power is above the temporal.

Secondly, if it were proposed to admonish them with the Scriptures, they objected that no one may interpret the Scriptures but the Pope.

Thirdly, if they are threatened with a council, they pretend that no one may call a council but the Pope ...

Now may God help us, and give us one of those trumpets that overthrew the walls of Jericho, so that we may blow down these walls of straw and paper, and that we may set free our Christian rods for the chastisement of sin, and expose the craft and deceit of the devil, so that we may amend ourselves by punishment and again obtain God's favour.'

Without doubt, it was the *Babylonian Captivity of the Church* which was the most offensive and heretical of Luther's writings in the minds of traditional Catholics. Even a liberal reforming Catholic like Erasmus exclaimed 'the breach is irreparable' when he read it. Drawing an obvious parallel to the seventy years of exile that the Jews endured at the hands of King Nebuchadnezzar, Luther argued that Christians has been held captive for hundreds of years by the false teachings of Rome on the sacraments.

Luther redefined what a sacrament actually was, rejecting the medieval idea that it is a ceremony of the Church which conveys grace. He insisted that the sacraments were commanded by Christ Himself and given by Him to the Church. Therefore, Luther rejected confirmation, marriage, extreme unction (the last rites), holy orders and penance, none of which were instituted by Christ. He did not deny they were legitimate ceremonies, but that they were sacraments. All of this was important because Luther was seeking to wrestle means of conferring grace out of the hands of the Church through the priesthood and to put it into the hands and hearts of ordinary believers through faith in Christ.

The two remaining sacraments were baptism and what Luther called 'the sacrament of the altar', what we would call communion. He claimed that Rome was at fault in three main ways in this sacrament. In the first place, communion should be administered as both bread and wine and not as the Catholic Church was in the habit of doing, keeping the wine only for the priest. Second, Luther rejected the thirteenth-century doctrine of transubstantiation which was an attempt to explain why the bread and wine still looked and tasted like bread and wine even though Christ had declared it was His body and blood. Finally, and most strongly of all, Luther rejected the notion that communion was in any way shape or form an offering for sin, since the Cross is a once-for-all sacrifice. Luther was well aware that his teaching on communion was likely to have his opponents jumping up and down declaring that his views are the same as those of Jan Hus and John Wycliffe who were both condemned for heresy the previous century.

Luther's heresies, according to his opponents, were almost too numerous to count. He had a false sacramental theology; he had rejected indulgences; he challenged the power of the Pope to excommunicate; he supported the views of notorious heretics who had already been condemned; he doubted the existence of purgatory.

Over and above all of this, however, was the issue of authority. Luther had rediscovered the authority of the Word of God. In doing so, he brought into question many of the practices and teachings of contemporary Christianity. Because the Pope was considered the spiritual successor of the Apostle Peter, his official statements were regarded as the very word of God, on a par with Scripture. In reality, this led to a marked divergence by the sixteenth century between Scripture and the practice of the Church.

In Luther's day the issue was papal authority. Today, the challenge to Scripture's authority is just as strong but comes in a different form. Some argue that contemporary culture simply makes whole portions of Scripture redundant. Liberal or 'post-evangelical' thinking is quick to ditch texts which are deemed to be politically incorrect or don't seem to fit with contemporary ethics. Both sixteenth century and contemporary opponents of the authority of Scripture essentially make the same cardinal error. They undermine the power of the Word of God by placing human reason above Scripture and ultimately this leads to false doctrine. For Luther, such an option was unthinkable. Hence he concluded his famous speech at the Diet of Worms thus:

'Unless I am convinced by the testimony of the Holy Scriptures or by evident reason – for I can believe neither pope nor councils alone, as it is clear that they have erred repeatedly and contradicted themselves – I consider myself convicted by the testimony of Holy Scripture, which is my basis; my conscience is captive to the Word of God. Thus I cannot and will not recant, because acting against one's conscience is neither safe nor sound. God help me. Amen.'

CHAPTER 7

THE BIBLE TRANSLATOR

'Here you will find the swaddling clothes and the
manger in which Christ lies'

LUTHER, ON WHY WE SHOULD READ THE BIBLE

In just four short years Luther had moved from being a loyal son of the Church to a heretic and outlaw in the German Empire. His life was in real danger and had been since the Diet of Augsburg in 1518. Following the publication of the 95 theses in October 1517, Luther had dramatically polarized European opinion. To many in Germany he was a national hero who offered religious, political and financial freedom. To religious conservatives he was a dangerous heretic who must be stopped at all costs. Charles V had granted him safe conduct to and from Worms and, as a man of honour, had kept his word. But what would become of Luther once the Edict of Worms,

Charles V's sentence condemning and outlawing Luther, had taken effect?

The Edict of Worms was not quite as life-threatening to Luther as it might first appear. Two of the elector-princes of Germany sympathized with Luther – if not theologically, then at least politically. Ludwig of the Palatinate and Frederick the Wise of Saxony refused to sign the Edict of Worms.

On 4th May, as he was on the way back to Wittenberg, Luther's party was intercepted by masked horsemen, who seemed to be highwaymen. They carried Luther away, and when he did not appear during the next few weeks, many assumed that he had been murdered.

As things turned out, they were agents of Frederick the Wise. Frederick wanted to give safe-keeping to Luther, but by staging this 'kidnap' he was able to deny all knowledge and involvement.

For the next ten months Luther was hidden for his own protection at the Wartburg castle near Eisenach. He was incognito. He grew his hair and a beard and called himself Junker (Knight) Jorg. Captivity in the Wartburg was, at the same time, both extremely difficult and incredibly fruitful. The sort of solitude and isolation that Luther experienced was potentially very damaging to his, or indeed to anyone's, spiritual well-being. 'I know the tricks he [the Devil] likes to play on me; he is a sad, sour spirit, who does not like the heart to be glad,' wrote Luther to describe the spiritual warfare, the blackness, he faced in this period of his life. As Luther tried to focus on the Scriptures he found the Devil doing everything he possibly could to distract and torment him. At one point Luther said that the Devil pelted the roof with stones, on another that he shook a sack of nuts and on another that he rattled around the stove. Luther even felt the Devil grunting evilly within him at one point and the result was some decidedly unpleasant and smelly wind! Eventually, Luther became so agitated that he threw an inkpot at the Devil – but hit the wall instead!

The battle, however, was not simply a spiritual one. It was also psychological and physiological. Luther was lonely and frustrated. Like Elijah after the Mount Carmel confrontation with the prophets of Baal (1 Kings 18), his loneliness led him to indulge in self-pity. Like Elijah, he had taken on demonically inspired opposition, but he now found himself plagued with self-doubt. He wavered between the feeling that he had been too defensive on the one hand and too aggressive on the other when he reflected back on his appearance before the Emperor at Worms. Could he have played things differently? Should he have? He was also physically ill, suffering from constipation and from insomnia.

Yet Luther's time in the Wartburg was not all doom and gloom. It was also one of the most fruitful periods of his scholarship. The solitude and lack of distraction enabled Luther to complete what was arguably his greatest scholarly achievement – the translation of the New Testament into German in only eleven weeks from December 1521 to February 1522. Other German translations of the Scriptures had appeared before Luther, but none can begin to compare. Luther turned a number of disparate dialects into a unified language to such an extent that he is often considered to be the inventor of modern German. He did for German what Tyndale (the translator of the first Greek to English New Testament) and Shakespeare did for English rolled into one. This Bible translation was not simply a phase of Luther's ministry. It became a lifelong devotion. The Old Testament did not appear in print for another twelve years after the New Testament. The whole work was continually revised and updated. Luther was continually looking to improve his work; the last printed page he saw before his death in 1546 was a proof copy of the latest version.

Luther went to extraordinary lengths to ensure the accuracy of his translation work. He investigated the crown jewels belonging to Frederick the Wise of Saxony in order to correctly translate the precious stones of Revelation 21. He consulted the local abattoir and butcher to accurately translate the animal sacrifices in Leviticus, persuading the butcher to cut up a sheep so that he could look at the innards! The New Testament was very much his work alone because of the enforced solitary confinement of the Wartburg. The Old Testament, however, was more of a collaborative effort. Friends who were also pastors, professors and scholars such as Philip Melanchthon, Justus Jonas and Johannes Bugenhagen helped form what today would be described as a 'translation committee.' Luther called it his Sanhedrin.

Luther's Bible was not simply an accurate translation, linguistically speaking. It certainly was, and to a remarkable degree by the standards and manuscripts available to him. But much more, it was a labour of love – a love for the Word of God and a love for the German people. His aim was to produce a Bible that was thoroughly German in every possible respect. Luther claimed that he had made Moses so German that no one would suspect that he was a Jew! Sometimes contextualization provided huge challenges linguistically, particularly in translating Hebrew poetry, notably the book of Job. The book, said Luther, suffered more under his attempts to translate it than did Job from the advice of his friends! Publishers and printers made fortunes from it. Luther never received a penny.

The order of books which Luther decided upon for his New Testament is usually surprising to the modern reader. Luther followed the principle of *treibt Christus,* or 'how Christ was taught', in other words, ordering the books by how explicitly they taught about Christ. Unsurprisingly, Luther gave maximum weight to the four Gospels and to the Pauline letters that were most explicit in their commitment to salvation by faith rather than works. Books like Hebrews and that 'epistle of straw' James which had a 'Jewish' and/or 'works' emphasis and flavour were put at the end of the canon, with other books like Revelation, of which he said 'in no way' was it possible to detect 'that the Holy Spirit produced it'.

Luther's aim in translating the Bible was to make Scripture accessible to the ordinary believer. The first

English Bible to be printed, the Great Bible, was published in 1539. Physically, it was a huge book which was fixed on a chain in every pulpit of every parish church in England. This was not a Bible for the lay person. It was a Bible for the parish priest. England was still a Catholic country.

Luther's Bible was an altogether different animal. It was a book that was easily transportable, a book to be read for personal edification and study. Luther's aim was to put the Word of God into the hands of as many people as possible. It is difficult to determine with certainty the impact of Luther's Bible translation on ordinary people in the towns and cities of Germany. Literacy rates were probably only at about 5% for Germany as a whole. However, we know that the first (1522) edition of the New Testament was published in a print run of five thousand. This was an exceptionally large run by the standards of the day. There was clearly an appetite for the Bible amongst ordinary people. Thousands of pamphlets and small books were printed all over Germany, not just by Luther himself but by a whole army of his supporters.

In 1524 Hans Sachs, for example, an evangelical poet, published his *Disputation between a Priest and a Shoemaker*. Ten further editions followed in 1524 alone. The tract is, of course, an imaginary conversation, but it reflects discussions that went on all over Germany at this time. The shoemaker is portrayed as knowledgeable in his handling of Scripture, respectful and polite. The priest, by way of contrast, is sloppy and ill-informed in his lack of Biblical knowledge. To have shoemakers, weavers, furriers and other humble manual labourers devouring Scripture would have been unthinkable ten years earlier.

Even those who were themselves illiterate were not necessarily devoid of Biblical knowledge. They could sit with others and hear preaching, have the Bible read to them and even commit considerable portions of Scripture to memory. Such a thing would have been inconceivable before the Reformation and Luther's Bible translation. It is no exaggeration to claim that Luther's Bible translation revolutionized Christian devotional practice in his own lifetime. This achievement still echoes around the world today. Today many of us almost take it for granted that our lives are changed day by day as we allow the Holy Spirit to renew our thinking and change our hearts through the reading of the Scriptures. But it was Luther who gave us as Christians the joy of direct access to the Word of God.

CHAPTER 8

AGAINST THE FANATICS

'You are my enemy...'

LUTHER

*'I desire to remain your enemy as long as you yourself
shall remain the enemy of God and of His truth'*

CARLSTADT

During Luther's ten months of enforced absence hidden in
the Wartburg, the Word of God faced another challenge
in Wittenberg from an unexpected quarter. The leadership
of the nascent reform movement had passed in this time
into the hands of Andreas Carlstadt (1486–1531), dean of
the Theology faculty at Wittenberg and Luther's debating
partner against Eck in 1519. At the time of Leipzig,
Carlstadt was as clear as Luther in his commitment to the
authority of Scripture. 'I will know of no other forgiveness

of sins than Scripture teaches,' he declared emphatically, 'no other word, no other holy writings, no other gospel … than that which the Holy Scripture contains.' In a tract *On Holy Water and Salt* (1520) he went on to say:

> *'I don't give much for what … popes have taught – it is the word of God that binds me and is dear to me, that throws all popes overboard, and that is our faith and none else.'*

With Luther off the scene, however, Carlstadt began to drive the reform movement in an increasingly radical and ultimately less biblical direction. It was also a direction which was extremely dangerous for the reform movement as a whole. Luther was now an outlaw and so the position of Frederick the Wise was an extremely dangerous one. At any moment Carlstadt's recklessness might precipitate armed intervention against Frederick from Catholic neighbours.

Nevertheless, Carlstadt drove the cause of reform at breakneck speed. Priests, monks and nuns began to marry, with Carlstadt taking the lead, marrying a young noblewoman of about sixteen. Communion was administered in both kinds and the Mass was recited in German.

For an ordinary Wittenberger this was a massive, even revolutionary, change. For hundreds of years the Mass had been recited in Latin and only the priest was able to drink from the cup that Christ had given to His disciples as he urged them to drink. Now the cup was freely available to all and the service was conducted in a language comprehensible to everyone.

Statues and images were destroyed as the role of the Virgin Mary and the saints as intermediaries was downgraded. They began to be described as 'idols', and therefore their presence in a church building as a breach of the second of the Ten Commandments. Canon law was deliberately and defiantly broken through the eating of meat on fast days.

Initially, Luther was supportive as he received news of events and sought to give advice from a distance. What Luther could not tolerate, however, were the claims of the 'Zwickau prophets'. Led by Nicholaus Storch, a weaver with no proper theological training or credentials, and strongly influenced by Thomas Muntzer (1489–1525), a dangerous radical who was ultimately committed to the destruction of the entire social order on 'Gospel grounds', the prophets claimed to have no need of the Bible but instead relied on direct revelation from the Holy Spirit. If the Bible were so important, they argued, God would have dropped it from Heaven. This rejection of the authority of Scripture led down a slippery sloope. Storch came to reject, for example, both communion and marriage, putting the whole spiritual and social fabric of Christendom into jeopardy. Unsurprisingly, this did not go down well with the Pope, the Emperor or Frederick the Wise.

Luther's colleague Philip Melanchthon had offered little resistance to Storch and the prophets. 'Who commissioned you to preach?' was the best he could muster; when the reply came 'The Lord God' he was pretty much lost for words. Frederick the Wise and the Wittenberg town council were greatly concerned but felt powerless to act. More and more Luther came under pressure to return. This was not merely a political, pragmatic or leadership issue. The emphasis of the prophets on the Spirit divorced from Scripture was a rejection of the Gospel and therefore of Christ Himself. There could be no greater threat to Christian faith.

Luther became so alarmed at the stories he was hearing that he decided, whilst still under imperial ban, to leave the safety of the Wartburg on 3rd March 1522 and return to Wittenberg. On his arrival home he was greatly dismayed by what he found. He preached eight times in the next week, arguing his case for Biblical solemnity in public worship. 'The Mass is a bad thing,' he agreed, 'but our first aim must be to win the heart, and to this end we must preach the Gospel.' Many were won back from the 'fanaticism' of the prophets. Carlstadt himself was unconvinced by Luther's arguments but patched up an uneasy truce only to quit Wittenberg a year later. The prophets were away from Wittenberg during this first week but, following their return, there was a stormy confrontation that led to their long-term departure.

Luther's confidence throughout this crisis, indeed, throughout his whole ministry, was in the power and authority of the Scriptures as the Word of God:

'Give men time. I took three years of constant study, reflection and discussion to arrive where I now am, and can the common man, untutored in such matters, be expected to move the same distance in three months? Do not suppose that abuses are eliminated by destroying the object which is abused. Men can go wrong with wine and women. Shall we then prohibit wine and abolish women? The sun, the moon and stars have been worshipped. Shall we then pluck them out of the sky? Such haste and violence betray a lack of confidence in God. See how much He has been able to accomplish through me, though I did no more than pray or preach. The Word did it all. Had I wished, I might have started a conflagration at Worms. But while I sat and drank beer with Philip [Melanchthon] and [Nicholaus von] Amsdorf, God dealt the Papacy a mighty blow.'

To paraphrase – what on earth did Carlstadt and his supporters imagine they were doing in destroying statues and stained-glass windows of the saints? It is much better, surely, to trust the power of the Scriptures to have its full impact in the hearts and lives of God's people. Let the Word of God have its sway rather than merely human agendas. Between 1517 and 1521 Luther's main priority had been to emphasize the authority of the Bible over tradition and a theology which had hidden the Scriptures and hedged them around with human accretions and misinterpretations. In the weeks after the return from the Wartburg he was pushing against Carlstadt and the radicals who undermine Scripture by adding to Scripture, not with human tradition but supposedly 'divine' extra-Biblical revelation. Whatever the threat from whichever end of the spectrum, Luther's response was the same – authority rests in Scripture alone.

CHAPTER 9

THE CHURCH BUILDER

'Anyone who is to find Christ must first find the Church.
How could anyone know where Christ is and what faith is in
him unless he knew where his believers are?'

LUTHER

Following the tumult caused by Carlstadt and the Zwickau prophets, Luther became more and more concerned to provide order and structure to his reform movement. Of course, nobody imagined in the early 1520s that the tensions that had erupted over the sale of indulgences in 1517 would result in a permanent division in Europe between the Roman Catholic and Protestant Churches. Admirers of Luther were simply known as 'Martinists', or as evangelicals. The word 'Protestant' was first used in 1529 to describe supporters of Luther who were 'protesting' against Charles V's attempts to impose the Edict of Worms, outlawing the new faith across the Empire. However, as the 1520s progressed, Luther began to provide increasing structure to the reform movement which would provide a context in which the new theology could flourish.

Luther's survival in the 1520s was almost entirely dependent on the political backing of Duke Frederick the Wise of Saxony. As time progressed, however, more princes committed themselves to the Reformation. Albert of Hohenzollern, Philip of Hesse, the Margrave of Brandenburg-Ansbach, the Count of Mansfeld, the Duke of Schleswig and the Duke of Brunswick all converted to the Reformation cause between 1525 and 1528. This led them to introduce Lutheranism as the 'state religion' in the territories which they ruled. German church services replaced Latin and they were not simply translations but rather significant modifications of the old version; German hymns were sung which set the Gospel to music and Luther's German Bible was read and preached from. These were massive changes in the worship experience of the Christian faithful. Their significance cannot be over-estimated. Church services were intelligible rather than just familiar to participants for the first time in centuries. The new evangelical communion service reflected the fresh understanding that it was not a good work or a sacrifice, not a re-enactment of Calvary.

Preaching was a hugely important part of the new Church order and of Luther's life in particular. 'If I could today be king or emperor,' Luther declared, 'I would not give up my office as preacher.' He often preached twice on Sunday and once during the week. Throughout his ministry he preached around three thousand sermons. In 1528 alone he preached on almost two hundred occasions. He was a truly great but not necessarily systematic preacher – that was much more the preserve of the 'Reformed' theologians, Zwingli and later Calvin. He was always God-centred, pointing to Christ as the fulfilment of God's promises. Preaching for Luther was a means of grace, for through preaching the Spirit takes the word and uses it to perform miracles in the heart of the believer as Christ is revealed. He set an example for others to follow in his hard work in the study in preparation for preaching, comparing himself to Moses in the desert striking the rock from which water gushed out:

'I beat upon Paul ... The Bible is a remarkable fountain; the more one draws and drinks of it, the more it stimulates thirst.'

For Luther, there was a close connection between his role in the University of Wittenberg and the task of preaching. He saw his doctorate in theology to be a call to teach the Word of God not simply to academic circles but the whole Church. Nevertheless, he maintained his focus on the academic world as a professor throughout his life and ministry both on a formal and informal basis. Admiring students from all over Europe came to study at Wittenberg. Fifteen came from the Netherlands alone from 1516 to 1520 and as Luther's fame grew more and more arrived from all over Europe. Some of those students even lived with Luther and his family. Their time together became known and recorded as 'table talks'. Students would sit for hours around the dinner table, asking him questions and recording their answers in their notebooks for future publication. During these discussions, Luther gave his wisdom on almost every conceivable topic under the sun. His comments are full of wit and colour. On death, for example, he remarked 'Therefore nothing were better for us than soon to be conveyed to the last dance and covered with shovels.' On another favourite subject, the Pope, he declared:

'[He] is a mere tormentor of conscience. The assembly of his greased religious crew in praying was altogether like the croaking of frogs, which edified nothing at all.'

Hymn singing was a particular innovation in Church life sparked by Luther and his followers. Luther's best known hymn *A Mighty Fortress is Our God*, a paraphrase of Psalm 46 was probably written sometime between 1527 and 1529. However, Luther's first hymn *A New Song Here Shall Be Begun* appeared as early as 1523 to commemorate the execution of two Antwerp Augustinian monks, the very first martyrs of the Reformation, who were burnt at the stake on 1st July in the same year. Luther's hymns were a hugely powerful tool to communicate the truth of the Gospel. They were sung in schools and homes but, first and foremost, they transformed congregational worship. A conservative estimate puts the number of copies of Lutheran and German evangelical hymns as high as 2 million over the course of the sixteenth century.

Given the opposition and persecution that Lutherans faced in this period, hymns were a vital source of nourishment and comfort for the believer. They instructed and inspired worship as an overflow of the heart. Simple language and rhyme were vehicles for children and adults alike to enable Paul's injunction to 'Let the word of Christ dwell in you richly' (Colossians 3:16) to be fulfilled. We should not be surprised at any of this. Time and time again throughout Church history a restoration of the authority of Scripture and of good doctrine has produced fresh expressions of worship – just as happened in England during the Methodist revival.

The imposing of an official Reformation was further strengthened by the outbreak of the German Peasants' War (1524–25). When war broke out Luther's initial sympathies lay with the peasantry. The demands of the peasants, as set out in the *Twelve Articles of Memmingem* (March 1525) contain clear evidence of Lutheran influence and some sort of 'Gospel mandate' for the uprising, in the minds of the peasants' leaders at least. They seem to have been particularly attracted to Luther's doctrines of the priesthood of all believers and Christian freedom, although they interpreted them largely within a socio-economic framework to justify the right of peasants to rise up against their feudal overlords. In his

Admonition to Peace (March 1525), Luther attacked the princes, nobles and bishops for their luxury, extravagance and mistreatment of the people. He rejoiced, like the Virgin Mary (Luke 1:52), that the Lord 'Has brought down the mighty from their thrones and exalted those of humble estate,' but encouraged the peasants to act 'justly and with a good conscience'.

Six weeks later, Luther was not nearly so sympathetic in his *Against the Murderous, Thieving Hordes of Peasants*. Using Romans 13:1 as justification, 'Let every person be subject to the governing authorities', he implored everyone who possibly could to:

> *'Smite, slay and stab, secretly or openly, remembering that nothing can be more poisonous, hurtful, or devilish than a rebel. It is just as when one must kill a mad dog, if you do not strike him, he will strike you and a whole land with you.'*

What had changed? The answer is straightforward – Thomas Muntzer. Muntzer was the most dangerous radical extremist in the Reformation movement in the 1520s. He combined some aspects of Luther's theology, particularly Christian freedom, with medieval mysticism. Most notably he developed a theology of 'divinisation' – that the work of God in the soul involves us as human beings taking into ourselves the divine nature of God Himself. He combined this with a justification of violence for 'Gospel purposes'; those who stood in opposition to the

Gospel should be slaughtered. This message potentially threatened the whole progress of the Reformation and therefore needed to be stopped, as far as Luther was concerned, at all costs.

In the explosive 1517–1521 period, Luther had an unswerving confidence in the undiluted power of the Word of God. 'The word of God did it all,' he had boasted. By 1528 Luther had adopted a more circumspect and realistic perspective. Between 1526 and 1528 teams were sent out into the parishes of Saxony to investigate the spiritual health and well-being of the population. They found a poorly educated clergy lacking theological training and ability, together with a lack of financial resources. Even more worrying was the lack of an even rudimentary knowledge of even the basics of the Christian faith amongst the laity. In the preface to his *Small Catechism* (1529) Luther pulled no punches in describing the woeful condition of clergy and laity alike:

'The deplorable, miserable condition which I discovered lately when I, too, was a visitor, has forced and urged me to prepare this Catechism, or Christian doctrine, in this small, plain, simple form. Mercy! Good God! What manifold misery I beheld! The common people, especially in the villages, have no knowledge whatever of Christian doctrine, and, alas many pastors are altogether incapable and incompetent to teach, so much so, that one is ashamed to speak of it. Nevertheless, all maintain that they are Christians, have been baptized and receive the

holy Sacraments. Yet they do not understand and cannot even recite either the Lord's Prayer, or the Creed, or the Ten Commandments; they live like dumb brutes and irrational hogs; and yet, now that the Gospel has come, they have nicely learned to abuse all liberty like experts.'

Luther's *Small Catechism* was aimed at children and his *Greater Catechism* at adults. However, both had essentially the same purpose. The essentials of the faith were identified as how a Christian ought to live (the Ten Commandments), what a Christian ought to believe (the Apostles' Creed) and how a Christian ought to pray (the Lord's Prayer). Each item was then expanded phrase by phrase in a way which was intelligible to children and adults respectively.

To a significant extent, the catechisms were born out of disillusionment. The Bible in undiluted form in translation made accessible and available to all had not delivered the results Luther had imagined possible back in the heady days of 1521. Scripture needed to be applied to the life of the believer. The *Small Catechism* was a tool for parents to teach doctrine to their children and was intended for children to commit Scripture to memory. Luther was, of course, the first writer in the history of the Church to come to this task as a father. He, unlike anyone before him, had genuine experience of answering the simple questions of young children in a way they could easily understand. The *Greater Catechism* contained what amounts to mini-sermons and was therefore a vehicle first for pastors to gain a grounding in Scripture and doctrine and then for them to communicate this clearly to their congregations.

Secular historians often minimize Luther's popular appeal both in Germany and overseas. It is often claimed that Protestantism was simply 'imposed from above' by princes for political reasons. This is only part of the story. It is certainly true that there were distinct advantages for a prince in converting to Protestantism. Henry VIII, for example, was at least partly motivated by ridding himself and England from foreign (Italian-papal) power when he finally moved in the direction of the Reformation. All over Europe the papal taxation (Annates) was particularly resented. It involved large sums of money being paid to Rome when a new bishop took office.

Luther's message offered rulers financial as well as political autonomy. When Luther published his *Address to the Christian Nobility of the German Nation* (1520), he tapped into the grievances of the German nation in a very conscious and deliberate way. He looked to the German princes and their frustrations towards Rome as a catalyst to propel the Church towards reform via a general council rather than through a weak and corrupt papacy.

But beyond the 'princely Reformation', there is plenty of evidence of Luther's popularity both at home and abroad. Luther's message, as we have already seen, had some appeal amongst the poorest and most illiterate sections of German society, the peasants. It was even more popular in the larger towns and cities of Germany, to such an extent that the Reformation has even been described as an 'urban event'. Over three-quarters of the larger independent cities of the Empire recognized the new Lutheran faith and over half became and remained Protestant. They did so because they were bowing to popular pressure. It was in the towns more than anywhere that people read, discussed and exchanged ideas on Luther's writings. Books like the *Freedom of the Christian Man*, with its emphasis on grace and faith in the life of the individual believer rather than sacraments administered through priests to the congregation at large, had a particular appeal in urban communities. Town councils, concerned above all else for law and order, opted for reform because it was what local people wanted, not because they were inherently Protestant as such.

Elsewhere in Europe the success of Lutheranism mirrors events in Germany. There was a Reformation which was 'imposed from above' and this was particularly the case in Scandinavia. A state Lutheran Church was established in Denmark in 1537. Religious toleration and Lutheran preaching was permitted in Sweden ten years earlier. Norway and Finland moved more slowly but in the same direction with state backing for reform.

However, this state-imposed reform is by no means the whole picture. The most urban area in Europe north of the Alps in this period was the Netherlands (modern-day Netherlands, Belgium and Luxembourg). It was here that Luther's message attracted its strongest support outside of Germany. This was despite the fact that the ruler of the Netherlands at this time was the arch-Catholic Emperor

Charles V. He ruled them, however, not through lesser rulers, as he did most of the Holy Roman Empire, but directly, as Duke of Burgundy. Charles was therefore not dependent on local princes like Frederick the Wise, who had turned a blind eye to Luther. He was able to enforce his policy of total hostility to Luther directly.

This meant that persecution was particularly intense in the Netherlands. The first martyrs of the Reformation were burnt at the stake in Brussels in July 1523. It was possible to be executed as a first-time offender in the Netherlands merely for the possession of a banned Lutheran book. This was no idle threat – martyrs and Lutheran books were both aplenty! Antwerp, a city of a hundred thousand, which was huge by early modern standards, was the most prolific printing centre for Luther's books outside of Germany. No less than forty books by Luther had been translated into Dutch by 1540 along with numerous evangelically orientated Bibles and New Testaments.

The peculiar circumstances of the Netherlands help explain both the success and the limitations of Lutheranism outside of Germany in Luther's own lifetime. On the one hand, Luther's message attracted significant support in the towns and cities, as in Germany, and particularly amongst the young and the well-educated. On the other hand, persecution meant that the abiding legacy of Luther was very limited.

In the 1550s Calvin would offer his followers in the Netherlands, France and other countries where evangelicals were persecuted for their faith, practical help and advice in how to plant churches. Luther was absolutely opposed to church-planting and was even reluctant to sanction small groups of believers meeting 'underground' for mutual edification and encouragement. He offered his supporters in territories where the ruler was opposed to the Gospel a simple choice – to come to Wittenberg or some other Lutheran part of Germany where they could practise their faith openly or to suffer martyrdom for the cause. An underground church was simply out of the question. This was not simply a theological standpoint for Luther. He himself had often risked martyrdom for the sake of the Gospel. Attendance at Worms in 1521 and particularly at the Diet of Augsburg in 1518 had carried a real risk of death, as had his return from the Wartburg in 1522 when he was under imperial ban.

Luther was always wary of radicalism and 'fanaticism'. He observed the explosive growth of Anabaptism in the early 1530s in the Netherlands and north-west Germany, with their theology of believers' baptism into a gathered community of believers, in horror. He was not unsympathetic to the plight of his supporters, but Luther had a strong theology of the Cross. There was, as far as he was concerned, no Gospel without suffering because the Cross is at the heart of the Gospel. In a curious sort of way, persecution and martyrdom was a good thing – it was a mark of the true Church, a vindication of the Gospel and a sign of the last judgment. The release of the forces of Antichrist showed the end of time had arrived and that Christ would soon return for His people.

CHAPTER 10

THE
FAMILY MAN

*'Does the pope set up laws? Let him set them up
for himself and keep hands off my liberty'*

LUTHER ON CELIBACY AND MARRIAGE

It is difficult for us to conceive of the radical nature of Luther's endorsement of marriage for the age in which he was living. For more than a thousand years the Catholic Church in Western Europe had advocated clerical celibacy and had thereby implied that celibacy was a spiritually superior condition to marriage. All this was to change in the 1520s.

The first clerical marriage of the Reformation took place in May 1521 when Bernhard of Feldkirchen tied the knot and Melanchthon wrote a pamphlet in his defence. A few weeks later in Wittenberg, Carlstadt published two tracts, one in German, *Instruction Concerning Vows*, and the other in Latin, *Against Celibacy in the Clerical, Widowed and Monastic Estates*.

Luther responded 'Not me!' when he first heard what Carlstadt was advocating. However, on reflection he then published his own tract, *Concerning Vows* (November 1521), which indicated that he too was moving in the same direction but with rather stronger Biblical arguments and exegesis that Carlstadt. In January 1522 Carlstadt himself married with two other reformers (Philip Melanchthon and Justus Jonas) as witnesses. Luther heard the news from the Wartburg and, somewhat surprisingly, expressed approval. There was not much that Carlstadt did in 1522 that Luther did approve of!

Luther finally committed in practical terms to marriage in 1525 when he was faced with the very practical problem of what to do with Katharina von Bora. She was a nun sixteen years younger than he was and had been placed in the nunnery when she was a small girl. Katharina was one of twelve nuns in a convent who, having read some of Luther's writings, were anxious to leave their confinement. Their flight was not without its dangers: the local ruler, Duke George of Saxony (bordering Electoral Saxony where Duke Frederick ruled and Luther resided), had had a clergyman executed when he decided to get married.

According to popular tradition, a merchant who delivered to the nunnery hid the nuns in herring barrels on a canvas-covered wagon and delivered them on Luther's doorstep upon their 'prison break'. A local student wrote to a friend: 'A wagon load of vestal virgins has just come to town, all more eager for marriage than for life. God grant them husbands lest worse befall.' Eventually, Luther managed to have all the girls returned to their parents or married off – save Katharina.

Katharina was due to be married to a man from a distinguished Nuremberg family but the parents of the prospective groom objected, presumably on the grounds that the marriage was beneath their son. Katharina herself, showing willingness to move on, apparently gave a couple of suggestions as to potential husbands for her: Luther's fellow professor Nicolaus von Amsdorf or Luther himself!

Initially Luther was not keen on getting married, despite being theologically convinced it was not wrong to do so. He still feared that he might be martyred for his faith and he did not want to leave a widow. Eventually, however, at the grand old age of forty-one (Katharina was twenty-five) Luther tied the knot on 13th June, 1525 in a small ceremony before witnesses, including fellow reformers Justus Jonas and Johannes Bugenhagen. Two weeks later there was a more formal public ceremony.

Marriage was a huge lifestyle change for Luther, as it is for any forty-one-year-old bachelor. 'One wakes up in the morning,' he said, 'and finds a pair of pigtails on the pillow which were not there before.' The first argument came over a wedding gift of twenty guilders which Martin wanted to refuse, because it came from Albrecht of Mainz, who had first permitted the sale of indulgences in Saxony. Katharina accepted because she was aware of a one hundred guilder debt Martin had brought into the marriage.

He also had some unpleasant bachelor lifestyle issues. Martin claimed that prior to marriage he had not made his bed in over a year:

'The straw was rotting from my sweat. I wore myself out with work during the day, so that I fell into bed oblivious of everything.'

However, the biggest adjustment in lifestyle was in the area of finances. Martin was, quite simply, hopeless with money. He was loath to accept payment for anything and quick to give away. In addition, he frequently invited his students to share the family home and never wanted to charge them anything for board and lodging. Katharina assumed responsibility and got the family finances on an even keel.

Katharina became the archetypal multi-tasking Proverbs 31 wife and, as such, she and Martin became something of a model Protestant family. She was responsible for children, animals and servants. At one time she had eight pigs, five cows, nine calves as well as a collection of chickens, geese, pigeons and a dog. She even ran a farm in Zühlsdorf which was a full two-day journey from Wittenberg. Luther was not entirely happy about this since it meant that any time Katharina spent there was time away from him.

The marriage was full of 'banter' and jesting. During one dinner table conversation, Luther reportedly said, 'The time will come when a man will take more than one wife.' 'Let the Devil believe that' came the reply, to which Luther answered, 'The reason, Katy, is that a woman can bear a child only once a year while her husband can beget many.' Still Katharina kept going citing 1 Corinthians 7:2, 'Each man should have his own wife.' To which Luther joked, 'Yes, "his own wife" and not "only one wife," for the latter isn't what Paul wrote.' It was Katharina, however, who finally ended the conversation by saying 'I'd rather go back to the convent and leave you and all our children' than be a polygamous wife.

Their mutual respect, however, was evident to all those who looked beyond the banter. Katharina was an intelligent woman and Martin acknowledged this by referring to her as 'Mrs Doctor' – whilst she invariably referred to him as 'Doctor Luther'.

One practical display of Martin's deep affection for Katharina was in his last will and testament which he wrote in his own hand. He made her his sole heir. This was almost unheard of in Saxony. It was normal practice for a man to make his children his heirs. They were then expected to take care of their surviving mother. But Luther wanted his wife to be economically secure and independent in her widowhood. Martin's love for Katharina can perhaps best be seen, however, in his nickname for his favourite book in the Bible, the letter to the Galatians in which Paul, full of verve and passion, sets out his case for justification by faith alone through grace alone. He called it, as the letter which was dearest to his heart, 'My Katharina von Bora.'

Luther was not the first married clergyman. Yet a former monk marrying a former nun was, at the time, truly scandalous. Popular superstition held that a two-headed monster would be the product of such a sacrilegious union. And the monk was Martin Luther, the infamous German 'heretic'. Within a few years, however, Luther was boasting, 'I have legitimate children, which no papal theologian has!'

Martin and Katharina had six children in all. Three boys, Hans, Martin and Paul and one daughter, Margarete all survived to adulthood. One infant daughter (Elizabeth) died before she reached eight months, which was a source of great distress to her parents. A year later, in 1529, another daughter, Magdalena, was born. Sadly she died when she was only thirteen years old.

As Magdalena worsened and death approached, Martin and Katharina sought to encourage Magdalena and each other through declaring their trust in God. Finally, Luther 'Fell on his knees before the bed and, weeping bitterly, prayed that God might will to save her'. The young girl died in her father's arms with her mother also in the room. They knew joy as a family and as a couple, but they also had their share of pain. Martin's epitaph, written for Magdalena but aimed primarily at consoling his desolate wife, expresses the heartache of a bereaved parent but also unequivocally declares his confidence in the Cross:

> 'I Lena, Luther's beloved child
> Sleep gently here with all the saints
> And lie at peace and rest
> Now I am our God's own guest.
> I was a child of death, it is true,
> My mother bore me out of mortal seed,
> Now I live and am rich in God.
> For this I thank Christ's death and blood.'

Because of Luther's huge importance in the history and

development of Protestant theology, there has been a tendency to want to sanitize him and to make him 'respectable'. One passage of a letter to his friend George Spalatin was removed from editions of Luther's letters because it was, quite frankly, too embarrassing, particularly for nineteenth-century editors of Luther's work:

> 'When you sleep with your wife Catherine and embrace her, you should think: "This child of man, this wonderful creature of God has been given to me by my Christ. May he be praised and glorified." On the evening of the day on which, according to my calculations, you will receive this, I shall make love to my Catherine while you make love to yours, and thus we will be united in love.'

One of Luther's most significant gains for the evangelical cause was his championing of the virtues of marriage and of sex. 'Whoever is ashamed of marriage', says Luther, 'is ashamed of being human'. Suggestions that marriage, and therefore, sex are somehow unspiritual is a slander and an attack of the Devil. Luther discarded the medieval notion that reason is 'high' and the physical is 'low' or base. The sex drive was, for Luther, a divine force, part of God's vital presence in man since man's physicality is part of his being made in the image of God. Faith, for Luther, is lived out in a physical experience and, thus, in his *Greater Catechism*, he explains the first line of the Creed thus:

> 'What I mean and believe is that I am God's creature, that

means that he has given me and continuously maintains body, soul and life, limbs small and large, all the senses, intellect and reason.'

No area of life should be thought of as unspiritual or unholy. Sexual desire and fulfilment are healthy and God-given. Thus, in his *Against the So-called Spiritual Estate* (1522) Luther explains:

'A young woman, if the high and rare grace of virginity has not been bestowed upon her, can do without a man as little as without food, drink, sleep and other natural needs. And on the other hand, a man, too, cannot be without a woman. The reason is the following; begetting children is as deeply rooted in nature as eating and drinking. That is why God provided the body with limbs, arteries, ejaculation, and everything that goes with them. Now if someone wants to stop this and not permit what nature wants and must do, what is he doing but preventing nature from being nature, fire from burning, water from being wet, and man from either drinking, eating or sleeping.'

In the Reformation Luther redeemed for us much of what had been lost in medieval Christianity. This was not just true theologically but practically. He restored dignity to everyday life. As far as marriage and sex are concerned, he took them from the 'unholy' and the 'dark hours of the night' and restored them as God's gifts to the Church.

CHAPTER 11

THE FLAWED CHARACTER

'I wish from my heart that Zwingli could be saved,
but I fear the contrary; for Christ has said that
those who deny him shall be damned'
LUTHER'S *TABLETALK*

In the early 1520s Luther was a living icon in the eyes of his many supporters. In February 1521 Aleander, the papal legate (ambassador) to the German court wrote to Cardinal Medici describing how copies of pictures of Luther as a saint were selling like hot cakes in Worms where Luther was about to stand trial. He stands in the picture holding a Bible open. Above him there is a halo and, above the halo is a dove, symbolizing the Holy Spirit. Two months later the Venetian ambassador reported, again from Worms:

'I cannot tell you how much favour Luther enjoys here. It is of such a nature that I fear it will produce some bad effect after the emperor departs and the diet breaks up, especially against the prelates of Germany. In truth, had this man been prudent and restricted himself to his first propositions and not entangled himself in manifest errors about the faith, he would have been not just favoured, but adored by the whole of Germany.'

Of course, the reality was somewhat different. Luther was a hero to many but even great men are deeply flawed.

One flaw that strikes many readers of Luther is his bad language. His earthy and sometimes downright crude language has often been ignored because it is embarrassing or misinterpreted as merely a product of his 'peasant' background and modest social status. Strange though it may seem to our ears, however, Luther did not swear because of his low social status but rather because he saw foul language as a weapon in his armoury against the Devil. For Luther one of the best ways to combat the attacks of the evil one is to swear at him, using crude toilet humour to pour scorn and heap abuse. The Devil does all he can to drag God's name through the mud. In return, Luther was happy to fight fire with fire, to fight dirty, as it were, by using foul language as a weapon of spiritual warfare!

The Apostle Paul's command 'Let no corrupting talk come out of your mouths' (Ephesians 4:29) leaves us at something of a loss as to how to handle a Biblical theologian's foul language. We can be tempted, somewhat snobbishly, to dismiss Luther's lifelong barrage of crude words hurled at opponents of the Gospel simply as a product of 'bad breeding'. However, Luther was well aware that he was engaged in a battle with a foe who is a slanderer and accuser of the people of God (Revelation 12:10). This being the case, he genuinely believed that one of the best ways of combating his slander was to go on the attack with the same weapon.

If Luther can be excused or at least understood for his slander of Satan, it is perhaps less comprehensible to us that he was equally abusive of fellow evangelicals. In 1527 Martin Luther wrote of Ulrich Zwingli that he would 'Rather drink pure blood with the Pope than mere wine with the fanatics' (*The Sacrament of the Body and Blood of Christ – Against the Fanatics*). How had two reformers united on so much ended up so fundamentally divided and in such hostility?

Luther and Zwingli met for the first and only time at the Colloquy of Marburg in 1529. The Colloquy was a theological debate with a political goal. There was a real danger of Charles V raising an army against the evangelicals (the threat did not actually become a reality until the Schmalkaldic War in 1546–47). Philip of Hesse, one of the leading Lutheran princes, was anxious to achieve theological unity which would then pave the way to a military alliance. Neither was achieved.

Luther and Zwingli had little or no expectation of success at Marburg. There was agreement on fourteen out of fifteen articles but there was never a hope of consensus on the Lord's Supper. Luther took the words of Christ's institution of the Lord's Supper 'This is My body' at face value whereas Zwingli believed that the word 'is' should be understood as meaning 'signifies'. According to eye-witness reports Luther simply wrote on the table either in beer froth or chalk dust (knowing Luther it was probably the former) *'Hoc est corpus meum'* ('This is My body') and that was that – deadlock!

In the earliest phase of his writing, most notably in the *Babylonian Captivity of the Church* (September 1520), Luther condemned the view that the Mass was a 'good work' or a sacrifice in no uncertain terms. Interestingly, he also spoke of 'signs' of covenant at this stage of his career such as the rainbow, God's covenantal sign to Noah, circumcision, God's covenantal sign to Abraham and bread and wine and the signs of the new covenant (*A Treatise on the New Testament, that is, the Mass*, August 1520).

In other words, Luther came very close to the 'Zwinglian' view that the bread and wine are not literally the body and blood of Christ but should be viewed merely as signs of the covenant, but he stopped just short. However, we must remember that the so-called 'sacramentarian controversy' – the rejection of the idea that the bread and wine of the communion service literally become the body and blood of Christ – had not yet occurred. The main focus of Luther's attack here was against the Catholic doctrine of the Mass as a sacrifice.

Zwingli came to his symbolic view of communion

through reading the work of a Dutch evangelical named Cornelis Hoen. Hoen had, in his reading of the Gospels, come to the conclusion that the bread and wine needed to be understood as 'signs' of God's new covenant promise and not as literal flesh and blood. In a similar way to a bridegroom giving a ring to his bride as an assurance of his love and as a sign of his covenant promise, so Christ gives Himself to His people in bread and wine.

In accepting this view, Zwingli was unwittingly embracing a theology that Luther had very deliberately rejected. Some months before Zwingli embraced this symbolic understanding of Hoen's, Luther had very consciously decided it was false.

On his return from the Wartburg he was greatly alarmed, as we have seen, by the 'fanaticism' of Carlstadt and the radicals. Carlstadt at this time had deliberately rejected any notion that the bread and wine became the body and blood of Christ. With some of the worst hermeneutics imaginable, Carlstadt had taken Matthew 26:26 'Take, eat; this is my body' and insisted that Christ in uttering these words had been pointing, not at the bread, but at His own physical body. Luther was appalled and not only rejected this specific exegesis but also any other symbolic interpretation of Christ's words.

When Zwingli published Hoen's ideas and endorsed them wholeheartedly, Luther saw the Zurich reformer as endorsing the errors of Carlstadt. Zwingli was therefore tarred with the same brush as Carlstadt and condemned as a 'fanatic'. The consequences of this for the evangelical movement as a whole across Europe were huge. The Reformation became permanently divided on theological grounds.

If Luther does not emerge with flying colours from the controversy with Zwingli he is surely at his least appealing and attractive in his anti-Semitism. In his pamphlet *Of the Jews and Their Lies* (1543) he writes:

'We must exercise harsh mercy with fear and trembling, in the hope that we could save some from the flames and embers. We must not avenge ourselves. They are under God's wrath – a thousand times worse than we could wish it upon them.'

Further, he urges:

'Firstly, that their synagogues or schools should be burnt down and what will not burn should be razed and covered with earth, that no man will ever see a stone or cinder of it again ... Next, that their houses should be broken and destroyed in the same way. For they do the same things there as in their schools. For that they can be put under a roof or stable, like the gypsies ... Thirdly, that all their prayer books and Talmudists, in which such idolatrous lies, curses, and blasphemies are taught, should be taken from them. Fourthly, that their rabbis should be forbidden, at the risk of life and limb, to teach from now on. Because they have lost their office for good reason ... Fifthly, that escort and road should be completely prohibited to the

Jews. For they have no reason to be in the country, being neither landlords, nor officials, nor peddlers or the like ... Sixthly, that they should be prohibited from usury and that all their cash and fortunes in silver and gold should be taken from them and put in safekeeping ... Seventhly, that young, strong Jewish men and women be given flail, axe, hoe, spade, distaff, spindle, and be left to earn their bread by the sweat of their brows ... For, as all can see, God's wrath over them is so great that gentle mercy will only make them worse and worse, and harshness little better. So away with them at all costs.'

Why did Luther express such animosity towards the Jews? First, because Luther stands in a long tradition and history of European anti-Semitism. The Jews must be hated by Christians, so the argument went, because they were 'Christ-killers'. Second, it reflects a growing pessimism in Luther. That was related to increasing grumpiness which, in part, was related to ill health and old age. But it was also in part due to a disappointment at a lack of progress of the Gospel. There is a marked shift in Luther's views on the Jews from his *That Jesus Christ Was Born a Jew*, which was published as early as 1523, and his *Of the Jews and Their Lies* which came twenty years later. Third, for Luther, the Jews were allied with Romanists and Papists, with the peasants of 1525 who had discredited the Reformation by misapplying Luther's teaching, and with the Muslim Turks. Together they comprised the forces of Antichrist that were a direct and very potent threat to the Gospel.

They were a part of a cosmic struggle between the forces of good and evil. They were on the enemy side.

Luther's writings on this subject cast a dark shadow over the Reformation. There can be no defence. His views are thoroughly shameful in every respect. Yet, even Luther in 1544 looked beyond the Jews to the sinfulness of the whole of humanity beginning with ourselves:

> *'Our great sin and sore misdeed*
> *Jesus the true Son of God, to the Cross has nailed.*
> *Thus you poor Judas, as well as all the Jews*
> *We may not upbraid inimically*
> *For the guilt is ours.'*

CHAPTER 12

THE LEGACY

'Not until I am gone will they feel Luther's full weight'

LUTHER IN 1531

When conservative-minded Catholics first voiced their horror at the implications of Luther's criticism of indulgences in 1517, Luther claimed that he was 'a loyal son of the Church'. He had no way of knowing at this stage the long-term impact of what he was unleashing when he nailed the 95 Theses to the church doors in Wittenberg. Even so, Luther's action on 31st October changed the course of history. Not just the Christian Church, but Europe and the world, look very different today as a result.

Not all of Luther's legacy was positive. Conflict between the Catholic and Protestant faiths unleashed a wave of religious wars throughout Europe in the sixteenth and seventeenth centuries. As Luther lay on his deathbed in 1546, his world was in chaos and there was every chance that the movement he had created would not survive.

Charles V, the Holy Roman Emperor, was, at last, after waiting sixteen years, poised for military victory against the Protestant military alliance of the Schmalkaldic League. By the end of the Emperor's reign, in 1555, the Lutherans had gained some legal recognition in parts of Germany through the Religious Peace of Augsburg. However, this peace was short-lived and lasted only to the Thirty Years War, which broke out in 1618.

A second negative impact of Luther's legacy was long-term division in the Church. Luther was not the first person to divide Christendom on theological grounds. Europe had already been divided between East and West (Orthodox and Catholic) for over four hundred years before the Reformation. However, the Catholic-Protestant schism was bitter and deep and the scars are still evident today.

Yet, whilst unity is precious, it must not be preserved at the expense of primary truth. There are some secondary issues where we can agree to differ as Christians. But there are others, such as the authority of Scripture and salvation through grace alone by faith alone, which are non-negotiable.

'Did God actually say?' (Genesis 3:1) has been the oldest and most dangerous question ever asked of the human race. When Luther answered this with a resounding 'Yes' and pointed to Scripture as opposed to Church tradition or ecclesiastical office, he re-established the Bible as the ultimate authority in matters of faith and doctrine. He rediscovered the power that God has vested in His Word. This basic conclusion was manifested in so many different ways in Luther's life and ministry. It can be seen in his desperate searching of the Scriptures, when he was a monk plagued with doubt and fear. It is shown in his dramatic speech before Charles V at the Diet of Worms in 1521, at the end of which he declared his absolute immovability – unless he could be convinced by Scripture (hence the title of this book). It is certainly borne out in his many hours of New Testament translation work in the Wartburg, and his lifelong devotion to the project of making the whole of Scripture available in the German language.

Second, and flowing from his fresh understanding of authority as he read Scripture, came Luther's rediscovery of the centrality to the Gospel of justification by faith alone. Catholic opponents of Luther found justification by faith alone impossibly offensive to their theological sensibilities. As far as they were concerned, Luther's theology allowed Christ to be united with a dirty, fornicating and promiscuous bride. Jacob van Hoogstraten, a Dominican theologian based at the University of Cologne expressed the horror of many of his contemporaries when he claimed that:

'[Luther] lists no preconditions for the spiritual marriage of the soul with Christ except that we believe Christ ... Not a single word is said about the mutual love by which Christ loves the Church ... Now what else do those who boast of such a base spectacle do than make of the soul, which is wedded to Christ in spiritual marriage, a prostitute and an adulteress, who knowingly and wittingly connives to deceive her husband and, daily

committing fornication upon fornication and adultery upon adultery, make the most chaste of men a pimp and a cowardly patron of her disgrace?'

Essentially, Hoogstraten, along with many other Catholic theologians, failed to understand the radical nature of what Luther was teaching. In his *Freedom of the Christian Man* Luther does indeed say that the union we enjoy with Christ is tantamount to a relationship between a king and a prostitute (the Old Testament book Hosea paints a similar picture).Through the wedding vow, Luther argues, the prostitute becomes joined to the king and all that he possesses becomes hers. She now shares in his royal identity and all her sin, death and judgment is taken by the king. Some people both in Luther's own time and today have been inclined to see 'Luther's Gospel' only as a message of 'forensic justification', that is, merely about being made righteous through a legal transaction which took place at Calvary, as Jesus takes our guilt and sin and His righteousness is imputed to us by faith. Seeing it only in these terms can make it seem purely technical and almost sterile. This can rob us of something of the joy and delight in the Gospel. Luther's message is also about relationship. Being united with Christ means that God is truly my Father and all the riches of the grace of a loving Father are now lavished on me because I am united to the Son.

In the medieval period the Church largely withdrew from and renounced the world. The full title of Thomas à Kempis' fifteenth-century classic, *The Imitation of Christ and Contempt for the World* exemplifies this mentality of retreat. To be a serious Christian in the Middle Ages meant to be a monk or a priest and preferably both! Luther swept this thinking away.

When he first took God seriously in 1505, Luther did so by entering a monastery. When he first encountered the holiness of God two years later it was as a new priest performing his first Mass. Luther thought and acted in this period like any other medieval man.

But Luther's new understanding of the priesthood of all believers and Christian freedom changed all of this. Sacrificing priests were turned into pastors and preachers of the Gospel. Lay people were dignified with an equal standing before God as those in ordained ministry. Ordinary manual labour became a spiritual activity. This reshaping of thinking also freed those ordained for ministry to marry and to raise children, as we have seen from Luther's personal experience. The gap between ministers and their congregations significantly narrowed.

Luther was even more radical in his treatment of monks and nuns. Such a form of spirituality was, for Luther, a distortion and a perversion of the very essence of Christian faith. His *Commentary on Galatians* (1531) gave him ample opportunity to launch some of his most virulent attacks on monasticism since this was, for Luther, just the sort of 'legalism' or works-based religion Paul was attacking:

'Of this difference between the Law and the Gospel there is nothing to be found in the books of the monks, canonists,

school-divines; no, nor in the books of the ancient fathers ... The schoolmen, the monks and such others, never felt any spiritual temptations, and therefore they fought only for the repressing and overcoming of fleshly lust and lechery, and being proud of that victory which they never yet obtained, they thought themselves far better and more holy than married men ... they put righteousness in the keeping of their foolish and wicked vows.'

Luther's emphasis on the authority of Scripture together with his rejection of priests as distributors of the grace of God through the sacraments helps us to understand the new importance he gave to the priority of preaching. Architecturally, any late medieval church was dominated by the altar. The Mass was a place where Heaven and Earth met. Christ was offered up as a sacrifice for sin through the words of the priest in the sacrament of the altar. In this and the other six sacraments, grace was administered to the Christian faithful by a priesthood. In contrast, Luther put the pulpit at the heart of the Church's ministry. Through the preaching of the Word, the grace of God penetrates our hearts and minds and faith is quickened in the unbeliever by the power of the Holy Spirit. Preaching is absolutely central to the communication of the Gospel for, as Paul says in Romans 10:14:

'How are they to hear without someone preaching?'

Luther saw himself primarily as a pastor and a teacher (or

doctor) of the Church. In retrospect he might be seen as 'prophetic'. Rather like Jeremiah was called by the Lord (Jeremiah 1:10) to 'Pluck up and to break down, to destroy and to overthrow, to build and to plant' Luther was as much a destroyer as he was a builder. In many ways, he was perhaps better at 'plucking up' than he was 'planting'! In his *Address to the Christian Nobility of the German Nation*, he compared his task of destroying false doctrine in the Church with that of seeing God bring down the walls of Jericho:

> *'May God help us and give us one of those trumpet blasts with which the walls of Jericho were overthrown to blast down these walls of straw and paper.'*

Much that Luther hoped for was not actually realized in his lifetime. Everything had seemed impossible in the heady days of 1519–1522. Rather as British soldiers went off to war in 1914 in the naïve optimism that 'it will all be over by Christmas', Luther imagined that the inherent rightness of his cause set against the false doctrine of Rome would mean a swift victory for the Gospel. In reality, it was more of a struggle – the sinfulness of the human heart coupled with the ignorance and spiritual darkness around us means that it would be more of a battle than Luther first realized. In a sense very little has changed. Twenty-first century Europe is just as dark, just as ignorant and just as sinful. Consequently there is just as much a need today for the sort of fearless proclamation of the Gospel as Luther made five hundred years ago.

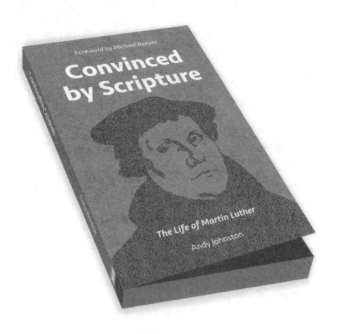

The Life of Martin Luther

Andy Johnston

a division of **10** **of those**.com

10Publishing is the publishing house of **10ofThose**.
It is committed to producing quality Christian
resources that are biblical and accessible.

www.10ofthose.com is our online retail arm selling
thousands of quality books at discounted prices.

For information contact: **info@10ofthose.com**
or check out our website: **www.10ofthose.com**